NEW ECONOMY

NEW ECONOMY

FLEXIBILITY, FREEDOM, REWARDS

Unique insights and observations. How the gig economy impacted the traditional economy and fueled an economy where the masses participate as owners in all models of distribution, engaging consumers differently... supporting the creation of a new economy of more INDIVIDUAL ENTREPRENEURS!

JOHN T. FLEMING
WITH ROBERT A. PETERSON
AND KATE GARDNER

RESULTS
FASTER!

PUBLISHING

Those who have a printed copy, use QR Code to access Safety Net Resources (https://safetynetresources.info) where digital formats of *NEW ECONOMY* are available free with one-time subscription to Safety Net Resources. Digital copies are not available through online bookstores. New Economy: Flexibility, Freedom, Rewards

ISBN: 978-1-7377320-4-4
LCCN: 2025922899

©2026 by Ideas & Design Group , LLC
Irving, Texas 75039

The purpose of this book is to enhance awareness. This book will inform and stimulate thinking. The contents of this book are not to be viewed as recommendations of any type.

Published by *RESULTS Faster!* Publishing in Flower Mound, TX

Printed in the United States of America

DISCLAIMER

The title of this book, which we describe as a perspective, may sound like we are about to dissect and explain what is different about the economy from an economist point of view. This perspective is not about how well we are doing as a U.S. Economy, nor do we make any attempt to discuss the metrics associated with the economy. The U.S economy remains the largest and most successful in the world.

A consensus of evaluation ranks the world's largest economies in the following manner:

1. United States   2. China   3. Germany   4. Japan   5. India

We are living and working differently. There are many changes in the manner in which we work and some of these changes are not only refining our definitions for work but also our definition of our economy. Our economy can no longer to be defined as it has been for the past 100 years.

The *NEW ECONOMY* is about the trends that have unfolded right before us and the innovation, change, and transformation we are now living. The *NEW ECONOMY* is also about the many choices that are available which enable Flexibility and Freedom in how we choose to develop careers, ensure that our incomes exceed our expenses, enabling our innate desire to live a life of purpose.

The *NEW ECONOMY* is about the people, the change in the way we view our relationship with working and living. In industrial economies, work is performed by workers who are generally in an employee relationship with the organization, corporation, or small business owner. The employee relationship is structured to provide the employee with a fair wage for effort invested. The organization or corporation then allocates enough gained from revenue collected from products and services provided to also pay the employee bonuses for good to exceptional performance and benefits that may include several types of insurance, profit sharing opportunities, training, and development support.

In the *NEW ECONOMY*, we envision more and more workers opting toward a hybrid approach to working and living meaning; flexible work will be embraced in addition to whatever type of traditional work one may be involved in. We also envision an increasing percentage of workers opting to pursue work that offers ownership, in whole or in part, of the work which fuels the growth of the Individual Entrepreneur.

The desire to be able to embrace flexibility and freedom in how work is not to be ignored or treated casually. In preparing this perspective, we have examined the gig economy in detail, its growth, and the factors which have fueled the growth.

The *NEW ECONOMY* is composed of every type of worker that one can describe from highly skilled to those with a desire to leverage their assets more effectively. The medical professional, legal professional, educator, and engineer are included. So is the artist and hobbyist, the parents looking to manage both family and work as they desire, not as they are required. Regardless of whether we explored professional freelancers or those seeking to complement an income, we found the essence of a *NEW ECONOMY*.

DEDICATION

To work with the ability to contribute passion and purpose, knowledge, and skills coordinated with the objectives of the work is considered to be the ultimate work definition. The objective of this perspective is to amplify the choices available with respect to how work can be accomplished. Work can no longer be defined completely with historical or traditional definitions.

We have to work! The questions are:

1. What type of work is most interesting to us and what do we need to learn about the type of work that inspires us?

2. How do we work? Do we aspire to be self-employed or employed by others? If you are age 35+, chances are your choices in terms of how you work were limited to two basic choices: Self-employed or employed by others. Today, there are multiple choices.

3. When and where do we work? The restraints of geography, which were once a critical part of the decision as to when and where we work are no longer barriers to new possibilities.

Today we view work as being in the following major categories.

1. Primary Career

2. Incremental income

3. Multiple income sources

4. Residual Income potential

5. Entrepreneurship – individual or traditional, small business or large business.

Traditional work in all formats will remain integral to civilized societies and mature economies throughout the world. The very idea of "work" in accordance to a defined need is simply a brilliant idea. Instead of one person attempting to do everything, which is actually impossible, work has been broken into segments/categories, sub categories, and micro categories of sub categories. Because civilized societies learned how to categorize and define work, we experienced continuous progress over time. Farming and growing crops was defined to be different than a study of the stars or the root causes of diseases and illness. Because we have been able to categorize work we have also learned how to optimize the results gained from the diverse types of work. We have progressed as a global society. We, collectively, have been able to progress the way we have due to our ability to define and focus in a very segmented manner.

This perspective is dedicated to the future of work and the new possibilities and opportunities that we now experience. I might add that the future for those of us who are already working is always NOW! I am honored to reflect upon the many evolutions and iterations that I have personally experienced regarding how work can be accomplished. I have had the experience of working in the traditional format, going to an office, and spending the greater part of my day in an environment that included many others who were also there to work. We worked the traditional hours of approximately 8:30 am to about 5:00 pm. Many of my friends worked different hours, some worked from 11:00 pm to 8:00 am. All of us had to find transportation to a fixed facility, allocate enough time to arrive on time, and generally, take with us some form of lunch and snack to help us get through an entire eight-hour work day or night.

There were always co-workers that we liked, and some were actually mentors because they had worked the job far longer than most within the work environment. Many in this category were recognized for their loyalty and rewarded for tenure with pins, plaques, watches, and gifts. This is what we now refer to as the traditional industrial economy model.

Today's economy is very digital, and technology plays a huge role in how we work. Because many Millennials have never experienced the perspective that I shared in the previous paragraph, many will not identify with the picture I painted. However, if you are Gen X, you certainly did.

Work possibilities, inclusive of Flexibility and Freedom to work when you desire, as much or as little as you want, become a possibility and an opportunity available to anyone who embraces what we might refer to as an entrepreneurial spirit: a desire to be more in control of how you work toward a positive outcome in your life inclusive of the ability to choose. I use a phrase to describe the preceding that is most appropriate to the possibility described: *Be the Architect of Your Own Destiny*! The possibility does exist.

Therefore, this perspective is dedicated to those who are choosing **Flexibility and Freedom** in how they work through new choices that are available. Freelancer, independent contractor, direct seller, agent, gig worker, and 1099 workers in all formats are critical components of the *NEW ECONOMY*.

ABSTRACT

The gig economy has become a popular subject in mature markets throughout the world, especially the United States. The words were used by the United States Congress when addressing the different classification of workers impacted by COVID-19. Since then, the gig economy has continued to become a new phenomenon attracting record numbers of people to the possibility of work that offers flexibility in how and where the work is being done. Some gig workers turn gigs into a preferred way of earning full time income. Many gig workers now find technology to be the enabler in turning underutilized assets, whatever they may be, into income earning opportunities. The choices in how we work, when we work, and where we work have never been greater! Information related to the gig economy, the definitions and understanding of gig economy, motivations for selecting and working a gig can be difficult to find; therefore, this book, the sequel to *Ultimate Gig* can help to eliminate misunderstanding and confusion when seeking to better understand the *NEW ECONOMY*.

NEW ECONOMY	Title	Description
Chapter 1.	Situation Analysis	Where are we? What Matters Most?
Chapter 2.	Gig Economy Growth	The three key drivers.
Chapter 3.	The Future of Work	Stats and facts.
Chapter 4.	*NEW ECONOMY*	A detailed look at what's new and different.
Chapter 5.	RELEVANCE is Requisite	What matters most.
Chapter 6.	Positive Trends	7 trends identified by the authors.
Chapter 7.	Direct Selling	Why direct selling should be explored.
Chapter 8.	The Voices	Real stories…
Chapter 9.	Authors Perspective	Summary & Outlook
Chapter 10.	Bonus-Strategic Mastery	Keys to living and working effectively by Tony Jeary
Chapter 11.	Recommended Support	Essential services to support Individual Entrepreneurs.

ACKNOWLEDGMENTS

NEW ECONOMY is what I describe as a sequel to *Ultimate Gig*. When I committed to do research to enable the writing of *Ultimate Gig*, I was motivated to do so by many close friends who knew me very well. When we wrote *Ultimate Gig*, we committed to a focus on better understanding the gig economy phenomenon and its impact on the definition of work. Consequently, *Ultimate Gig* was about a change in the way work was being done. *Ultimate Gig* never identified a sole choice of ultimate gig work/participation. The new choices were far too many and the benefits of participation were perceived very differently by the many diverse segments of the population.

We looked at the gig economy phenomenon from a perspective based upon stats and facts, not emotions or opinions, or what we thought might be happening. Included in the book were interviews with a few C-level Officers of direct selling companies who were known to realize that the marketplace was changing. These executives also realized that direct selling models might be headed toward adjustment, refinement, even innovation and transformation.

Today, a few years later, we have witnessed a lot of innovation and transformation. Also included in *Ultimate Gig* was a chapter solely focused on the impact of technology and legal challenges. *Ultimate Gig* was not a self-help book designed to be inspirational or motivational; however, it may have provided both.

PayQuicker is an innovative global financial technology company that provides its clients with robust payouts and treasury solutions. For over 16 years, PayQuicker has leveraged its time-tested and award-winning technology to revolutionize payouts and serve the diverse needs of over 300 clients and millions of payees across industries. Having extensive experience empowering payouts in the gig economy, PayQuicker contributed insights to our book: *Ultimate Gig—Flexibility, Freedom & Rewards*. PayQuicker also sponsored, in part, the largest research study that we conducted on the gig economy which is republished in this book in Chapter 2.

NEW ECONOMY is approached in the same manner with similar objectives to the work we published in *Ultimate Gig*. However, the new work represents approximately four more years of observation and study. The gig economy has continued to grow as forecasted in the first edition of our work. Gig economy Compound Annual Growth Rate (CAGR) continues to track at 16%+ and this growth rate is now forecasted to possibly continue beyond 2034. The impact on mature economies around the world is simply amazing. Gig participation is expected to be around 50% of all workers reaching a total participation in excess of 100 million by year-end 2027 in the U.S. alone. Many qualitative assessments note that participation of gig workers in China may have already exceeded 200 million.

Work of this nature is not possible without the contributions of many. It is acknowledged that every conversation with a few hundred people along with the treasured conversations with close friends have contributed to the insights that are shared in *NEW ECONOMY.*

I have spent most of my working career involved directly or indirectly with the direct selling channel of distribution. However, the thoughts shared in this book have been accumulated from diverse experiences that started in architectural school and collective observations, research, and study. In architectural school we learned quickly that every design does not become a building. The design of the building is always completed before construction starts and, if construction starts before every detail is completed, rapid refinement and adjustment becomes critical otherwise the construction process could be stopped, and the building could fall or never reach completion. Architecturally designed buildings are designed and then built to withstand the test of time. Buildings are not built to stand for a few years.

The goal to consistently achieve sustained growth and withstand the challenges over a period of time is mastered by few, pursued by all … individual, organization or business in any format. Relevance does not last forever. Individuals can stop growing and never achieve happiness and peace of mind, not to mention success. Organizations, non-profit and for profit can fail to achieve their goals to withstand the challenges faced and the efforts embraced to achieve consistent, sustainable growth. Even the Church can go out of business. No individual, organization, school, or business model is immune from becoming irrelevant.

This book is not about "how to." It is about sharing thoughts, reflecting on observations, research, insights, and experiences that will stimulate the best of thinking. Wherever you are at this moment in time, you are in the right moment. This simple belief has enabled me to understand and seek learning in my disappointments. One of the greatest at inspiring us to think differently was the author, teacher, and inspirational speaker, Jim Rohn. His work and articulation of principles, values and concepts will forever be etched in the minds of anyone taking time to become familiar with the man and his messages. Those who have experienced Jim Rohn in any format, will remember one of his most famous messages: "*For things to change, we have to change.*" I altered the quote by using the word "we" vs the word "you." The meaning of the quote remains the same.

I hope that the experiences shared in this book will stimulate your thinking.

Enjoy!

> *"And whether or not it is clear to you, no doubt the universe is unfolding as it should. Therefore be at peace with God, whatever you conceive Him to be. And whatever your labor and aspirations, in the noisy confusion of life, keep peace in your soul. With all its sham, drudgery, and broken dreams, it is still a beautiful world. Be cheerful. Strive to be happy."*

— Max Ehrmann © 1927

ARCHITECTURE OF BOOK

INTRODUCTION/
REFLECTIONS

In 2017, we committed to researching the gig economy. In the first quarter of 2018, our original Gig Economy Project Team, and a small group of dedicated advocates of the direct selling method for distributing products and services agreed to contribute and sponsor the project. Our research was focused on gaining more insight into determining the key drivers of gig economy growth and why so many people were participating – approximately 50 million in the U.S. at that time. The gig economy had received the attention of economists, researchers and consultants including the largest and most notable business consulting firms in the nation. When we realized that the United States Department of Labor was beginning to recognize the existence of gig workers, and the gig phenomenon, we knew we had to pay attention.

Our first publication (magazine format) was distributed in June 2019. This work was titled: *"Welcome To The Gig Economy."* Our objective for this publication was quite simple: Alert the world to the fact that the growth and appeal of the gig economy was not a fad, it was the beginning of redefining how we view work. Dr. Greg Marshall, Rollins College – Winter Park Florida, contributed an article to the first publication which focused on defining the different personas of those participating in the gig economy. That original article was later expanded in *Ultimate Gig,* the book. That article remains as relevant today as it was when first published. The manuscript for the first edition of *Ultimate Gig* was completed in 2020 and published in the fall of 2021. At that time, most of the world was considered to be in recovery mode from the worst pandemic we had experienced in over one hundred years.

During the early phase of my life, the study of architecture consumed my passion and purpose because of my fascination with structures and buildings. However, it was marriage and the need to earn more income to satisfy lifestyle aspirations that initiated my involvement with a direct selling company. With the experience gained working as a direct seller, with my wife and then as an executive, I witnessed firsthand the benefits to be gained from working in a manner whereas flexibility and freedom become foundational to the work. Through my experience with the direct selling model, I also realized that my passions, purpose, personal principles, and values were transferable and could be aligned with another type of work.

As you continue to read this book you will gain, perhaps, more insights as to why it makes sense to leverage underutilized assets into additional income sources, especially when we can. The gig economy, the result of innovative technology which enables simplicity, has changed the game! Flexible work is no longer a desire; Flexibility in how we can work is now accessible and a choice. Many diverse types of work can be accomplished when, how, and often from where we want to do the work.

The term "gig economy" was popularized by some of the first companies to attract attention. Uber and Lyft disrupted the transportation industry by duplicating a taxi or limousine type service by providing ordinary people with an opportunity to convert their underutilized assets including time into an income earning opportunity. Airbnb is now recognized as being one of the largest hotelier's in the world, however, they do not own hotels.

Defining the gig economy is important to understanding the perspectives that we share. The gig economy is much more than a label used to reference part time work. The biggest incorrect perception we have encountered over many years of observation and study is the perception by others who reference the gig economy as an army of Uber/Lyft drivers. Gigs are categorized into four major categories: Transportation, Services, Selling and Leasing. Under each category there are thousands of possibilities, some are familiar to most and some are new. Professionals of diverse descriptions can be described as gig workers including freelancers, consultants, agents, educators, doctors, attorneys, engineers, graphic artists, etc.

Some types of gig work require physical presence and specific allocation of time. Many other types of gig work support those desirous of freelancing their experience, knowledge, and skills, even passion and/or purpose... at any time or any place. Technology can be said to be the enabler. Work can be done from home, office, living room, park bench, smartphone, even the beach. You can choose the way you desire to work and make the decision yourself! Professional or non-professional, skilled or relatively skilled. When you know how to do something that is of value to others, you gain more control of how you use your time when you know how to leverage what you have as an asset. Regardless of whether you are young or mature, you can find a gig or multiple gigs, possibilities, and opportunities, which can be the beginning of a more entrepreneurial approach to life and work. In the *NEW ECONOMY* in which we now live, the individual can complement primary sources of income and create new income streams accelerating the attainment of goals enhancing the way we live and work.

xxvi | NEW ECONOMY

Summary Insights:

- *Ultimate Gig* was published at a time when the gig economy was first recognized as a workforce phenomenon vs a growth in part-time work participation.

- The growing number of independent workers was estimated to be at 50 million U.S. participants in 2020. Today, most estimates put gig economy participation to be approximately 70 million.

- *Ultimate Gig* told the story! The emergence, growth and appeal of the gig economy represented a new trend toward the desire for more flexibility and freedom in how work can be accomplished.

- *NEW ECONOMY* will tell a new story. The new story represents what has transpired since 2020 and what can be expected. There is a major shift that has occurred…the masses now have more control over who owns the work.

The gig economy has redefined how work can be done. It has also become a **Safety Net** for those who are displaced and replaced without warning. The Mature can work a gig as easily as a Millennial or Gen Z. It makes no difference. Personal choice as to how we work is abundant. The consumer is also a king or queen. The way consumers act, and purchase products and services, determines whether companies remain relevant in the marketplace. No longer do we have restrictions as to where we can shop or when we can shop. The store hours are 24/7 and the location is not geographical because the store is a digital platform.

An online digital platform can be a recognizable brand that we know a lot about, or it can be a new brand that we are looking to become acquainted with. Once we gain trust, we may make a purchase. When we do, chances are we may be purchasing because of the influence of an intermediary who made it possible for us to know about the new brand and its products and services.

A new equalizer is born into our society. People from all walks of life can now participate in the distribution channels of products and services as intermediaries and be compensated for their sharing of experiences and influence. **This is the *NEW ECONOMY*!**

We are now enabled as individuals with more choices than we have ever experienced. We do not have to be dependent; we can be independent. As bold as the previous assertion may be, the possibility is much greater than ever before. This belief triggered an interest in understanding the phenomenon of the gig economy however, as a result of better understanding the gig economy, we now realize; the gig economy triggered our ability to leverage underutilized assets and activate EQUALIZERS and possibilities that never ever existed before. The gig economy has fueled the growth of the *NEW ECONOMY*.

The benefits of the historical industrial economy work model are numerous. Great companies, including government agencies have developed using this model and people from all walks of life have been beneficiaries. In the traditional industrial economy work model, the owner of the enterprise providing the work opportunity owns the work. The owners of the work also own the opportunity to hire in accordance to the guidelines established by the company. Owners of the work also retain "exclusively" the ability to increase wages and/or promote the employee to higher levels of responsibility. The owner of the work also has the ability to terminate the arrangement when warranted as long as the decision does not violate basic rules of engagement and fairness typically found in the company's guiding principles or the laws which govern, to some extent, the manner in which the company conducts its business.

Approximately ten short years ago, legendary business consulting companies such as McKenzie, Gartner and Deloitte started to publish articles related to the "Future of Work." Approximately fifteen to twenty years ago, Human Resource professionals started to experiment with "flextime" which gave birth to the flexible worker – a worker who did not work the traditional working hours of forty hours per week while maintaining the employee/employer working relationship.

The *NEW ECONOMY* blends and embraces the attributes of flexibility and freedom in how work can be accomplished. Historically, the company, government agency, organization or the small business created by an entrepreneur, were the sole owners of the work. In the *NEW ECONOMY*, the game has changed again. **NEW ECONOMY workers are more entrepreneurial creating the emergence of more and more individual entrepreneurs.**

This book is really about sharing with you what we have learned and experienced through our work, perhaps, stimulating your thoughts. We are experiencing the most favorable marketplace for the independent entrepreneur that we have experienced in over one hundred years. If you are already involved in any type of individual entrepreneurial activity such as leveraging your assets to create additional income, you will find this book to be a reaffirmation of your pursuit. You may also realize that your personal marketing position will be reinforced from the information you will absorb. For those who are seeking to better understand your choices and the pathways that you might pursue, this book will definitely provide the background to stimulate and support your thinking and decision-making process.

Our Understanding of You

You are reading this book because you are seeking to better understand new possibilities which are available or you are already participating in the *NEW ECONOMY*. Gaining control of the way you work and earn complementary income or new income via the creation of new or multiple income streams is a possibility for you. As you read the book, we suggest that you explore your mental thoughts always reminding yourself of "what matters most to you!" Keep the following types of thoughts in mind. In the *NEW ECONOMY*, people from all walks of life will become more of the architects of their own way of working and living...when they choose to do so.

What Is Your Purpose?

We perform better when we are of clear purpose as to "why" we do what we do. A clear purpose becomes high octane fuel. A clear purpose serves to inspire, motivate, and encourage your exploration. The possibilities are exciting, and they are available.

> *Millionaire Alexis Ohanian walked out of the LSAT 20 minutes in, went to a Waffle House and decided he was "gonna invent a career." He founded Reddit.*
>
> —*Preston Fore, Business writer for Fortune*

A Few Reminders

1. **The Speed of life** has accelerated exponentially. Much has changed and continues to change relative to how we do just about everything.

2. **The internet** is no longer an option; it has become essential to all aspects of life and work. Therefore, access to the internet is critical to how we function and whether we are effective and successful in the way we live and work.

3. **Using technology** is now a way of living and working. What was complex to us 20 years ago is now embraced and mastered by 10-year old's who cannot imagine life without a smartphone.

4. **The smartphone dominates**. Most reports indicate 4+ billion smart phone users in the world. The average amount of time spent using the phone is 3.5 hours per day. Americans spend 5.4 hours per day using their smartphone. That is a lot of time on a device. We are now dependent upon our smartphone.

5. **Flexibility** matters to all of us. We no longer wish that life and work were more flexible. Flexibility is more of a choice than ever before. Life and work can be designed around schedules, routines, and responsibilities. We can actually choose to seek, explore, and exercise our ability to choose the way we would like to live and work.

6. **Education** remains important. Learning opportunities are available 24/7. We no longer have to wait on a classroom or an instructor to learn more about something we desire to gain more knowledge about. This will become more and more important to free societies throughout the world. The internet enables education.

7. **Self-Employment is a possibility.** The United States of America is often thought of as the birthplace of free enterprise in its finest forms; however, over the past 100 years we have been more of an industrial economy based upon rigidity in how we work.

8. **We are experiencing a renewed interest in self-sufficiency, entrepreneurship, being more in control of how and when we work.** The emergence of the gig economy is proof.

9. **We are living and working in a digital economy** based upon interaction with digital platforms, which connect us with what we need and desire.

10. **Credit means debt** and debt is not an asset. As you will note in a later chart that we will present, savings amongst Americans may be lower on average than you may have thought. The relationship between earnings and expenses may be the single most crucial factor which impacts on our level of happiness and peace of mind.

11. **The concept of insurance will be redefined**. The concept of insurance in all formats was designed to insure against loss of something. A stronger and more powerful form of insurance is emerging as "assurance." Assurance focuses more on what can be done to assure the vision and hope of a healthy and prosperous future.

12. **Public Policy Makers** will struggle to protect old norms while supporting innovation simultaneously.

13. **Corporations and organizations** that demonstrate relevance will thrive. Individuals will play more of a role in whatever role they play, many will be independent while remaining interdependent on the company or organization.

14. **Microentrepreneurs** are emerging at a faster rate than employment opportunities.

15. **We desire more control of our life/work balance.**

CHAPTER 1
SITUATION ANALYSIS

The Situation Analysis that we provide in this book is very similar to the situation we described in *Ultimate Gig* (Emerald Publishing 2021). The way we work continues to evolve in definition. The future is always coming faster than we think and all of us are always participating in the invention of the future.

Our first chapter is designed to provide you with background and context. For many, the gig economy has been more about more choices to earn money quickly. Earning quick money has its place, as millions seek and engage in such opportunities for short-term objectives. In this book, we will define the emergence of possibilities that are far beyond the tactical and task focused short-term effort which activates quick rewards and payment.

Thanks to continued advances in technology, we can now work flexible hours from a location of choice, earn a complimentary income, or build a career from freelance work and/or entrepreneurial choices. Technology is also bringing us the incredible tool of Artificial Intelligence (AI) which enables us to do much more, much faster. Collaborating with a bot is no longer a far-fetched idea. In fact, those of us who write are using a bot all the time as the artificial intelligence identifies our incorrect use of words or punctuation and offers corrections/suggestions instantly.

As technology continues to evolve, the options will continue to expand for both work flexibility and the rewards received for time invested, thus allowing for a more robust definition of work. What started out as subtle waves of change have grown to be seismic shifts in the structure of the world of work. From our perspective, we are both a witness and participant in the creation of a *NEW ECONOMY* whereas the worker has more ownership of how, when, and where the work can be completed. This shift in the way we define work also fuels the rise of the Independent Entrepreneur. In this book, we continue to examine the gig economy however, the observations and study of the past five years enable new insights.

The financial reasons for seeking flexible work are as strong as they ever were and are undoubtedly a key driver in the *NEW ECONOMY*. However, there is much more to the new possibilities than the opportunity to earn complimentary income in a flexible manner. The ability to work when you desire fulfills needs, making it easier to juggle work and childcare, the opportunity to create another income stream, leverage underutilized assets, or gain the experience of being an independent entrepreneur. Younger generations consider flexibility essential in the work they choose. The ideal job, or the way we work, is no longer confined to a definition associated with eight hours per day five days per week.

The Industrial Revolution created significant wealth for a small percentage of the population. This era was known to be "asset heavy." In the *NEW ECONOMY* that is emerging, companies that we put into a gig economy category are "asset light" representing a significant shift in how products and services are marketed and how intermediaries and consumers are engaged.

"At the turn of the 20th century, almost half (50%) of the compensated U.S. workforce was self-employed. By 1960, this number shrank to less than 15% because of the Industrial Revolution. It is also highly likely that the self-employed constituted more than half of the compensated workforce at some point prior to 1900. For the 50 years since 1960, the percentage of self-employed in the U.S. economy has been approximately 10%."

Note: Quote is attributed to Tom Peters first used in 1993.

It is evident that our U.S. economy has been dominated, for over 100 years, by large corporations and a very traditional form of work – eight hours per day, five days per week owned by a select few. America and most mature economies were built on the creative ingenuity of entrepreneurs. The *NEW ECONOMY*, in many ways, is viewed as a restoration of entrepreneurship and control. In the *NEW ECONOMY*, the masses now have new opportunities to own and control the work or some portion of the work.

Gig Providing Companies Fueled the *NEW ECONOMY*

In conventional jobs, the company recruits a full-time workforce. You are generally required to be physically present at the place where the work is conducted in order to complete your assignment. On the other hand, under the gig economy umbrella, you can find work without commitment to a physical facility.

Gig providing companies like Uber, Lyft, Task Rabbit, Thumbtack, Fiverr, Upwork, and so many others focus on providing the worker with flexibility. These companies do not make significant investments in assets. Instead, they use technology to connect expertise and assets with consumers or potential clients who need the products or services offered by independent contractors.

Adam Smith, the 18th-century philosopher often recognized as the father of modern economics and a major proponent of free markets, posited the belief that "left to their own devices, people will always act in their self-interest, and those interests will inadvertently level out to create the best outcome for all." Smith felt that a free marketplace would serve to support the creation of better and higher-quality products and services. We see these ideas at work within the gig economy and especially in what we describe as the *NEW ECONOMY*.

Gig workers often improve the quality of the service being rendered. Many gig economy providers and workers solicit immediate feedback from their customers. Consumers rate their service providers via an app that makes a simple request once the transaction is complete. The consumer is asked to rate the service provider with one to five stars. There is no waiting for the traditional quarterly, semiannual, or annual performance appraisal typical of conventional jobs. The service, product, and the worker are evaluated immediately. In many cases, the gig provider also rates the consumer. This straightforward process serves to encourage higher quality all around.

The gig worker participating in the Etsy global online marketplace (www.etsy.com) can be located anywhere in the world and market their products around the globe through the Etsy platform. Etsy has more than 6.6 million small business owners/independent contractors involved and has become one of the most popular global online shopping malls. Etsy ads can now be found on many national and global television channels. Etsy is just one example. The gig choices available are very numerous.

Our research reveals that there are thousands of gig opportunities, perhaps many multiples of such a figure. The impact on labor statistics is staggering and game changing. Approximately 30%

of the current labor force participates in some type of gig, and we are rapidly approaching a 50% participation rate within a few years here in the United States (U.S. Department of Labor). We find estimates that as much as 80% of the current labor force may be receptive to gig work. The most important insight to be gained from our observations of the gig economy are the elements which are attracting so many people from all walks of life. The facts are: Simplicity in the manner in which an income opportunity is offered and engaged is attractive. Your ultimate selection of an income opportunity may not be considered a gig from your perspective. However, we now find that gigs have gone upscale and new creative approaches to personalized health care are a perfect example. Health Care Professionals including Medical Doctors participate in delivering these personalized services at home or in the office. These opportunities are considered gigs.

Traditional definitions may define gigs as part-time jobs, but they are much more! A part-time job differs from full-time employment in the number of hours worked and the benefits received. In the past, part-time work opportunities have been associated with a willingness to work for hourly wages less than the hourly wages earned by those in an equivalent full-time job. The gig economy does not recognize these rules.

By our definition, a gig offers flexibility and freedom in how, when, and where one does the work for rewards that are basically cash-based and quickly paid. The gig participant is a micro-entrepreneur, an independent contractor, his or her own boss. Also, it is essential to understand that the gig economy is a new phenomenon in its infancy. As we continue the journey through this book, discussing various aspects of the gig economy and what might be most important to you as a current or future gig provider or gig participant, we expect a continued evolution.

Gig providers, participants, consumers, local and national regulatory agencies will continue to unveil challenges and opportunities which will be addressed, we believe, to further create what we describe as the *NEW ECONOMY*. The amount of income earned via gig work includes the value placed on flexibility and freedom enjoyed; therefore, a comparison of gig opportunity earnings with hourly earnings of any type is not a valid comparison. Some hours of gig work will yield more than others in terms of cash rewards, but flexibility also has an intangible value. Gratuities are a very important component of the income many gig workers receive for the service rendered. This encourages a focus on quality benefiting both the worker and the provider.

There are four major categories of gig work:

- **Transportation**

- **Services**

- **Selling**

- **Leasing**

From our perspective and for purposes of this book, gigs fall into one of the four categories that we have shared. These four categories are generally used by those who are researching and writing about the gig economy. The number of gig opportunities within each category are too numerous for any one book. However, understanding the four categories can be helpful to those seeking to understand where talents, skills, and experience may fit. The gig providers within each category provide what we also refer to as a platform. The term platform arises out of the technology focus all gig-providing companies bring into play. They have created digital platforms in which the connection between the provider of a product and/ or service with a client or consumer who needs the product or service can be easily connected. The gig providing companies, through their platforms, are more effective and efficient in making the connection between provider and consumer.

Transportation Gigs enable the possibility of using a car to facilitate income earning possibilities. Once engaged with your gig provider, the use of an app typically enables you to work when you want to. Simply turn the app on when you want to work. Turn it off when you are done for the day. The income earned from transporting people and products to specific destinations could change an asset (your car) that was basically a debt into an income-earning possibility.

Service Gigs provide a different type of opportunity. Your skills can become a solution for those who need something done that they cannot do themselves, or do not want to do themselves. Service gigs also include any type of service whereas the owner does not want to employ a full-time worker, they prefer a gig worker/independent contractor who makes themselves available when needed or desired. There are many Service Gig Providers. A quick online search will reveal the possibilities.

Selling Gigs enable possibilities never ever imagined less than 20 years ago. The digital platform is the new store. No longer do we have to drive across town and invest many hours in looking and searching for just the right item. A few minutes of online search can provide access to many possibilities. We have choices at our fingertips. Using our fingertips does not require a tank of gas, the crowds of a store, or a series of interviews.

New platforms like Shopify, Etsy, and others have emerged that allow individuals to market their products and services with the professional support of a digital presence which can be an equalizer. The newest business can compete effectively with a more established brand via a very effective and appealing digital presence. Social media platforms allow for interaction with friends and potential customers who may have an interest in what you are providing. When contact is established and interest activated in purchasing your product or service, it is all accomplished online. Fulfillment of the order is easily outsourced. Once a digital presence is established, the business is now open 24/7.

Leasing Gigs are also popular. What Air BnB started has now expanded to just about every possibility that you can imagine. Underutilized tools can be leased/rented, rooms and/or homes, vacant lots, and even cars. With Turo, anyone can basically rent their car, which is often parked, and be just like Hertz or Avis. Hertz, Avis, Enterprise, and others are no longer the only brands that rent vehicles. An exotic car might be available for the weekend, and it may be an Independent Entrepreneur/Gig Enthusiast providing the opportunity.

CHAPTER 2
KEY DRIVERS OF GIG ECONOMY GROWTH

- Cultural Shift

- Vast Advancements in Technology

- Economic Realities

We are experiencing a cultural shift in attitudes and expectations, vast advances in the way we use technology, and a clearer understanding of economic realities often covered up by statistics such as employment or unemployment rates that do not measure the quality of life. When we decided to initiate our research on the gig economy several years ago, we became most interested in how we got to this new place and why gig work has become attractive. As we stated earlier, approximately 70 million are participating in the gig economy in the United States alone and that number is expected to exceed 100 million in a few short years.

Behind every new phenomenon are forces that have fueled the changes/shifts. This is undoubtedly true for the growth and appeal of the gig economy. Times have changed and so have cultural attitudes. The growing number of participants in gig work is driven by the desire to experience more freedom and flexibility in how the work is done. Younger generations consider these attributes to be essential. Half of all freelance gig workers consider their gig(s) their career. Women have long appreciated work opportunities that can be accomplished during hours that are flexible and controlled by the worker, not an employer. Older workers who have been replaced or displaced in traditional jobs, or who found retirement different than what they imagined, also seek work that offers flexibility and freedom. Retirement is no longer thought of as a specific moment in time.

Quality of life and being able to sustain a quality of life is most important. Technology changes the game! It does not take a lot of research to understand that technology has played a considerable role in the growth and appeal of flexible income earning opportunities. The mobile phone has been around for a long time; however, our phones certainly got a lot smarter over the past 15 years, a period synonymous with the continuous growth and popularity of the gig economy. Technology has provided us with new tools and amazingly effective ways to communicate. Technology makes engagement and participation so much easier for both gig providers, gig workers, and consumers. The trust factor which contributes to the success of the transaction will play a huge role as we continue to learn more about artificial intelligence and the role that bots will play in our lives.

The opportunity to control how and when you work, with the support of a brand that provides useful marketing which often connects a worker with a consumer, becomes very appealing. Peter Diamandis, states in his book, *The Future is Faster than You Think*: "Our biggest companies and government agencies were designed in another century, for purposes of safety and stability. They were not built to withstand rapid radical change." Technology has become disruptive in an incredibly positive manner. We can now do more with less and invest less time experiencing the productivity we desire. Technology changed the game and helped fuel the growth of the gig economy. With new inventors and visionaries like Peter Diamandis, Elon Musk, Bill Gates, Jeff Bezos, Richard Branson, and a host of others, who are consistently investing their wealth in shaping the future, we expect technology to continue to play a significant role in shaping the growth of the *NEW ECONOMY*.

In our research and study, I have personally had many "holy cow" moments. You, too, will experience the same. Technology is having a dramatic effect on the way we do just about everything. We communicate differently therefore we market our products and services differently. Consequently, we work differently.

Economic realities are also key motivators for seeking incremental income possibilities. We are living in a paradox. In the United States, while it may be the best of times for some, it is also a challenging time for many. Those who are attempting to increase the quality of life, take care of themselves and their families, enjoy some of life's wonderful opportunities such as owning a home, eliminating debt, paying for college education, taking vacations, and investing in future retirement, it is a challenging time. Reliance on traditional wage increases when inflation rates can exceed the percent of expected wage increases creates a loss in real purchasing power. Credit card debt is growing here in the U.S. and the amount of money saved from wages earned is shrinking.

Economic Realities

U.S. Credit Card Trends

Credit Card Debt Over Time

2000-2024 (Weekly, Seasonally Adjusted)

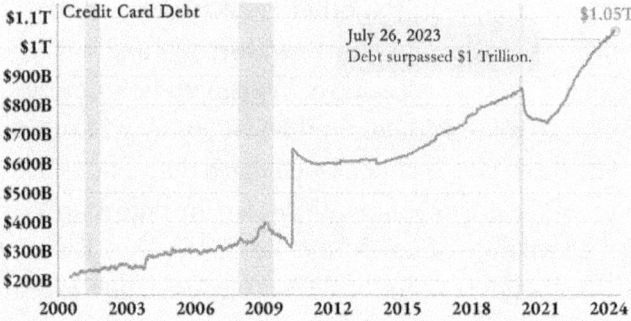

Credit Card Debt

July 26, 2023
Debt surpassed $1 Trillion.

$1.05T

$1.1T
$1T
$900B
$800B
$700B
$600B
$500B
$400B
$300B
$200B

2000 2003 2006 2009 2012 2015 2018 2021 2024

Interest Rates on Credit Card Plans

2000-2024 (Monthly)

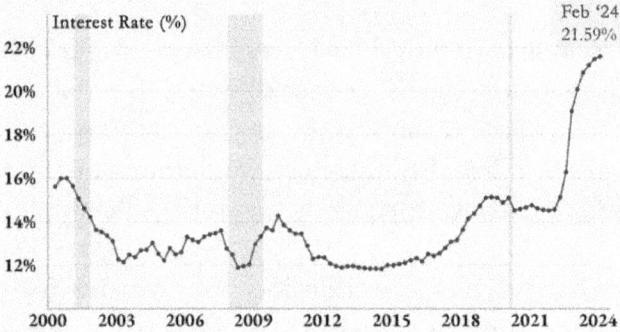

Interest Rate (%)

Feb '24
21.59%

22%
20%
18%
16%
14%
12%

2000 2003 2006 2009 2012 2015 2018 2021 2024

FES Product of Forensic Economic Services   Data: FRED

Half of the population spends more than their income

(Monthly income after tax MINUS average monthly expenditures)

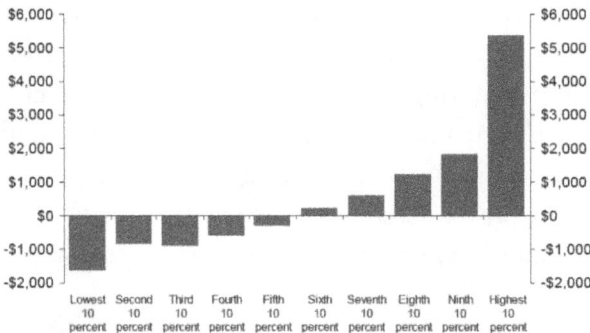

$6,000
$5,000
$4,000
$3,000
$2,000
$1,000
$0
-$1,000
-$2,000

Lowest 10 percent | Second 10 percent | Third 10 percent | Fourth 10 percent | Fifth 10 percent | Sixth 10 percent | Seventh 10 percent | Eighth 10 percent | Ninth 10 percent | Highest 10 percent

Source: BLS Consumer Expenditure Survey 2018, DB Global Research

More Stats and Facts

Average Amount Saved	Gen Z	Millennial	Gen X	Baby Boomer
$1,000.00 - $10,000.00	63%	61%	49%	34%
$10,000.01 - $25,000.00	8%	9%	8%	9%
$25,001.00 - $50,000.00	8%	9%	10%	5%
$50,000.01 - $100,000.00	8%	7%	9%	8%
$100,000.01 - $250,000.00	3%	4%	13%	11%
$250,000.01 - $500,000.00	1%	2%	3%	8%
$500,000.00+	2%	4%	4%	16%

Source: Forbes Advisor Get the data Embed According to our survey, roughly 28% of Americans across all four generations currently have less than $1,000 in personal savings, including emergency funds, non-workplace retirement accounts and investments. With the average national rent price sitting at $1,372, having less than a grand tucked away means many Americans are teetering on the edge of financial instability, with little cushion to absorb unexpected expenses.

Undoubtedly, age plays a big role in the amount of savings one has—older generations typically have more money saved, as they've had more time to accumulate wealth. Our survey found that the majority of Gen Zer's (54%) and Millennials (52%) have less than $5,000 saved, compared to 42% of Gen X respondents and 29% of Baby Boomers.

Unsurprisingly, the oldest generation—Baby Boomers—have amassed the most impressive savings balances. Our survey revealed that around 17% of Baby Boomers have more than $500,000 saved, while that figure dwindles to just 4% among both Gen Xers and Millennials and a mere 2% among Gen Zer's.

Key Stats and Facts

Average Wage Increases 2024 vs 2023	Hourly – 1.2%
	Nominal – 4.2%
Forecasted Inflation Rate 2025	2.9%
Growth in Gig Economy (2024 vs 2023)	16% Est
Percent of Consumers interested in starting a business	23%
Companies engaging Part Time Workers and Independent Workers	Part Time – 50%
	Independent – 33%

Summary Insights

When we first started our research on the gig economy, the questions and various points of view were very interesting. Many thought the gig economy to be a temporary fad more so than the beginning of a major change in the way we value flexibility and freedom. Through our analysis of factors influencing gig economy expansion—both in terms of participation and company-level revenue growth—we concluded that this trend represents a significant and enduring transformation, rather than a temporary phenomenon.

As we now write the manuscript for *NEW ECONOMY*, the gig economy has performed precisely as it was predicted to perform. The Compound Annual Growth Rate (CAGR) has been consistently positive based upon aggregated searches of information easily found on the internet. Our latest round of research (all data) and a comparison to earlier research is published in the next chapter.

The value of Flexibility and Freedom in how we work is a precious freedom. When flexible work becomes available in various formats, it makes sense for the wise to explore the possibilities. When underutilized assets – physical assets or the personal assets of time, knowledge, skills, experience, passion and purpose, can be converted to positive income earning possibilities, the humanity of the workforce is attracted. Men and women participate in the gig economy because they seek more control of the work that must be done to live the lives we desire to live.

CHAPTER 3

THE FUTURE OF WORK/GIG ECONOMY STATS & FACTS

Introduction and Brief Background

This chapter presents the results of research sponsored in part by PayQuicker, an innovative financial technology leader in the global payouts market, in conjunction with the Ultimate Gig Research Project. The research reported here, which is based on surveys conducted in July 2020 and April 2023, is a component of the years-long Ultimate Gig Research Project, a program dedicated to empirically and systematically assessing trends in the "gig economy" to inform and improve both business and public policy-related decision making.

Most unique about the findings of the research conducted in 2023 is the accuracy of the data revealed and the continuous growth of the gig economy further fueling the growth of what we now refer to as the *NEW ECONOMY* of Independent Entrepreneurs.

During the time period represented by the 2020 and 2023 research there were major changes that took place in the economy and in society. Chief among the changes were the accelerating mobility of the population and changes in work behaviors and locations due to the COVID-19 pandemic. For example, according to Census Bureau and Pew Research Center reports, in 2021 nearly 7.9 million Americans moved from one state to a different state, and in 2022 a majority of individuals who could perform their job functions from home did so through telework. The consequences of such changes have impacted the gig economy in numerous ways.

The "gig economy" is an umbrella term that encompasses subsets such as the "sharing economy," the "on-demand economy," and the "platform economy." Recent estimates peg the gig economy at more than $1 trillion annually in the United States, with an average annual growth rate of 16%-17% and projected to involve nearly 100 million gig workers by 2027.

At its essence, the gig economy is a channel mechanism for effectively and efficiently linking gig workers and their customers. Gig workers that populate the gig economy are independent contractors who primarily pursue part-time income opportunities and are typically compensated using pay-for-performance criteria. Collectively, surveys conducted for the Ultimate Gig Research Project present a comprehensive portrait of self-identified gig workers that captures their heterogeneity. This gig worker heterogeneity and the heterogeneous nature and rapid growth of the gig economy have major implications, not only for business but for government and society as well, especially when considered in the context of the COVID-19 pandemic and the digital labor platforms that operate within the gig economy. These implications include redefining the concept of, and compensation for, work; adopting and adapting gig-based business models; and assuming responsibility for training workers and compliance with government regulations.

Although a plethora of research has been conducted on the gig economy, much of this research has focused on firms offering an online labor platform, such as Uber or Air BnB, or on a particular subset of the gig economy, such as the sharing economy. Similarly, research on gig workers has typically been limited to specific categories of workers, such as 1099 workers, direct sellers, or transportation providers. Such workers are merely disparate subsets of the gig workforce. To date there has not been a comprehensive study of gig workers as they define themselves. Indeed, virtually no large-scale research project has been conducted to identify gig workers generally, document their gig-related behaviors, and investigate their demographic characteristics and motivations in a form useful for business decision makers and public policy officials.

This research gap simultaneously reflects an absence of information as well as a surfeit of misinformation regarding gig workers, to the detriment of everyone concerned with the gig economy. The 2023 survey represents the most recent round of empirical research conducted on the gig economy under the Ultimate Gig Research Project. As such, it updates insights from prior surveys and provides insights into the nature, scope, and growth of the gig economy and the gig workers who participate in it. Of particular interest is the analysis of individuals who pursue multiple gig activities.

Key Research Findings

The Appendix to this chapter summarizes the research methodology and presents selected questions and responses. In this chapter the survey results are briefly described under three headings—**The Structure of Gig Work**, **Gig Earnings**, and **Gig Worker Heterogeneity**. The next section of the chapter contains some practical implications of the research.

The Structure of Gig Work

According to the 2023 survey data, about 40% of the gig workers in the United States reported working one (and only one) gig in the past 12 months, slightly down from 45% in 2020; 28% reported working two gigs and 32% reported three or more gigs (i.e., a "primary gig" and one or more "secondary gigs"). The latter two percentages slightly increased from 2020 (in 2020, 24% of gig workers reported working two gigs and 31% reported working three or more gigs). One potential implication of this shift is that many gig workers may have less time and effort to spend on a particular gig or to allocate across a combination of gigs in 2023 than they did in 2020. Regardless, the shift in number of gigs worked requires further research.

The insert below provides detailed responses to the number of gigs-worked questions. In brief, the tendency toward working more than one gig suggests a possible trend that needs to be explored.

Percent of Sample

Number of Gigs Worked	2020	2023
1	45%	40%
2	24%	28%
3	9%	9%
More than 3	22%	23%

Changes in Gig Activities

Although there was a tendency for gig workers to work more than one gig in 2023 compared to 2020, relatively more significant changes took place in the types of gig activities pursued. This is illustrated in two distinct ways.

- First, certain gig activity concentrations changed from 2020 to 2023. For instance:

- ◦ In 2020, the most popular gig was professional services (e.g., accounting, law, consulting); nearly 16% of gig workers reported working in this activity category. In 2023, the corresponding percentage was about 6%.
- ◦ In 2023, the most popular gig was delivery services (e.g., restaurant meals, groceries, errands), with about 13% of all gig workers participating in this activity category. This compares with slightly in excess of 6% of all gig workers participating in the activity category in 2020.
- ◦ The percentage of gig workers offering home repair or other manual skill-based services increased from almost 7% in 2020 to slightly more than 13% in 2023.

- • Second, individuals working multiple gigs were somewhat more likely to work their gigs in the same activity category in 2023 than they were in 2020. Thus, for example, ridesharing or transportation service gig workers were more likely to work for both Uber and Lyft in 2023 as compared to working for Uber and having a graphics design gig in 2020. Generally,

  - ◦ In 2020, 27% of the individuals with more than one gig performed their gigs in the same activity category.
  - ◦ In 2023, 34% of individuals with more than one gig performed their gigs in the same activity category.

  For example, in 2023 gig workers pursuing home repair activities in particular tended to work multiple gigs in that activity category. Fifty-five percent of the survey participants with a primary home repair gig also worked on a secondary home repair gig.

Table 1 below details the percentages of gig workers pursuing either one gig or a primary gig if they had multiple gigs in fourteen gig activity categories investigated in the 2020 and 2023 surveys.

Table 1

Type of Gig (Only/Primary Gig)	Percentage Response	
	2020	**2023**
Ride-sharing or other transportation service	5.1	8.2
Restaurant meals, groceries or other delivery or errand services	6.5	13.3
Child-care or elder-care services	6.4	7.2
Graphic design, photography, writing, or copy editing	6.0	4.2
Home repair or other manual skill-based services	6.8	12.6
Selling products or services that you make or provide yourself	10.8	12.6
Professional services (e.g., accounting, law, consulting)	15.5	6.4
Free-lance computer work including data entry and website development	10.1	5.5
Pet care, personal assistance, yard maintenance, house cleaning, house-sitting, or other personal services	7.9	10.1
Selling or representing products through a direct selling or network marketing business	5.2	2.3
Selling products or services that are made or provided by others but not through a direct selling or network marketing business	4.2	4.9
Publishing videos, blog posts, or other content online and receiving affiliate marketing commission, advertising revenue, sponsorship fees, or other pay	2.1	2.6
Short-term real-estate rental or instant hotel services	1.4	1.5
Renting other personal property (e.g., boat or RV)	1.3	0.7
Taking online surveys and gaming*	NA	2.0
Other (for Primary Gig) (please specify):	10.7	5.9
Sample Size N=	1,001	2,019

*New Category Added for 2023

Comments

In 2020, a plurality of the gig workers surveyed, 41%, reported that they worked their gigs by means of an online platform, whereas a third (34%) worked offline; the remainder worked their gig(s) through an online/offline combination. To obtain a slightly different perspective on online platforms in the gig economy, the 2023 survey delved into how gig workers used "digital tools." About one-quarter of the gig workers surveyed in 2023 did not use any digital tools; about one-sixth used digital tools exclusively, with no interpersonal interactions. The remaining gig workers surveyed used digital tools in conjunction with personal customer and client interactions. Thus, media depictions of gig workers as primarily individuals connected to, or dependent on, an online platform (especially one related to ridesharing) are not completely accurate.

While the *absolute number* of individuals working a particular gig type or specific activity in 2020 may not have substantially changed in 2023, individuals entering the gig economy since 2020 are pursuing different gig pathways that in turn impact the *percentages* of gig workers in the activity categories. For example, whereas the *number* of people working a professional service gig may not have changed from 2020 to 2023, but because many individuals who entered the gig economy subsequent to 2020 pursued a delivery gig, the *percentage* of gig workers working professionally declined. These results possess numerous implications. In addition to showing the overall structure of the gig workforce, the results may also suggest that gig workers are amenable to changing activities, may be variety-seeking, or more to the point, may be more opportunity-seeking than previously acknowledged.

Consider again, as an illustration, delivery service gigs. It is well-established that the pandemic and the concomitant move to work from home stimulated the desire for, and growth of, home delivery of groceries and restaurant-created meals. As a consequence, there was a need for gig workers to make deliveries, and whereas some existing gig workers undertook additional delivery activities, new workers entered the gig economy specifically to meet the demand for home deliveries. This entry caused the percentage of workers pursuing a delivery gig to double from 2020 to 2023.

Gig Earnings

Perhaps the most persistent topic of interest in the gig economy relates to gig earnings. Gig work is driven by freedom, flexibility, and intentionality, which also translates to the manner in which gig workers expect to be paid. How much do individuals expect to earn from their gig(s), and how much do they actually earn from their gig(s)? How much time do gig workers spend on their gig(s)? How do gig workers use their earnings, and how are they paid? Interestingly enough, and commensurate with the notion of a gig being a part-time activity, and contrary to what the mass media disseminate, individuals enter into gigs with realistic expectations and aspirations regarding possible earnings. (See Appendix 1 for details.)

In general, the median annual household income of gig workers is somewhat below the median household income in the United States. Furthermore, the annual household incomes of individuals pursuing a single gig in 2023 appeared to be slightly less than those of individuals pursuing multiple gigs. See the income distributions below for individuals pursuing only one gig, 2-3 gigs, or more than 3 gigs.

Annual HH Income	One Gig	2-3 Gigs	>3 Gigs
Less than $17,999	18.3%	13.6%	14.5%
$18,000-$49,999	32.9%	34.3%	30.8%
$50,000-$99,999	32.2%	34.9%	35.2%
$100,000 or more	16.7%	17.3%	19.3%

Moreover, consider the following:

- On average, slightly less than one-quarter of the gig workers surveyed in 2023, 23%, expected to earn less than $100 per month when starting their gig. This percentage has not changed from 2020. Another quarter expected to earn between $100 and $299 per month when they started their gig. Hence, approximately half of the gig workers surveyed expected to earn less than $300 per month when starting their gig. Less than 3% of the gig workers surveyed in 2023 expected to earn $4,000 or more per month when they started their gig.

- These numbers can be compared to what gig workers reported actually earning. In particular, about 44% of the gig workers surveyed reported earning less than $300 per month, which suggests gig workers in general actually earn slightly more per month than they expected to earn when starting their gigs. More to the point, approximately 80% of the gig workers expecting to earn less than $100 per month actually earned less than $100 per month from their gig.

- About two-thirds of the gig workers surveyed earn about what they expected to earn when starting their gig. However, this relationship differs as a function of gigs worked. Whereas 65% of the survey participants with only one gig earned about what they expected to earn, and 69% of the survey participants with a secondary gig earned what they expected to for this gig, only 57% of the survey participants earned what they expected to earn with respect to their primary gig.

- About 45% of the gig workers surveyed in 2020 indicated that gig work contributed less than 10% of their annual household income, while a similar 43% of the gig workers surveyed in 2023 indicated that less than 10% of their annual household income came from gig work.

- About one-third of the gig workers surveyed typically work 4 to 8 hours per week on their only or primary gig, and this time allocation has not changed from 2020. Gig workers with more than one gig tend to spend more time on their primary gig than gig workers with only one gig, but less time on their additional gig(s) than they do on their primary gig.

- Moreover, as might be expected, the most important reason people took on a gig was that they "needed more money." Across gigs, 45% of the gig workers surveyed said this is why they pursued their gig(s). Other reasons for engaging in a gig included:

  ◦ Enjoy the work (18%)
  ◦ Had available time to work (9%)
  ◦ Allowed greater flexibility (9%)
  ◦ Permitted diversifying income stream (7%)
  ◦ Exploring different interests (7%)

- When asked, "How do you primarily use the money you earn from your gig?," 49% of the gig workers surveyed in 2023 stated that they used their gig earnings to pay household bills. This percentage is a significant increase from 2020, when 37% of the gig workers surveyed stated that they used their gig earnings to pay household bills. At the same time, whereas 31% of the gig workers surveyed in 2020 reported saving or investing their gig earnings, the corresponding percentage in 2023 was 20%. This shift in allocation from savings/investing to bill paying appears to be reflected in the gig activities pursued in the different years and differences in gig worker characteristics. Other uses of gig earnings (e.g., improving personal lifestyles, supporting children, etc.) were fairly consistent across gigs worked and time.

- In line with the nature of gig work, about 40% of the gig workers surveyed in 2023 were paid immediately upon finishing their gig. An additional 12% was paid every day.

The most frequent form of payment was cash or check. Thirty-nine percent of the surveyed gig workers were paid this way; an additional 34% was paid by direct bank deposit, and 24% was paid through a mobile wallet, cash app, or the like. Forty-six percent of gig workers with only one gig were paid directly by their customers or clients. This percentage increases slightly to 52% for gig workers with two or more gigs. Eleven percent of the gig workers surveyed in 2023 were paid through a third-party payment provider.

- The importance of immediate pay for performance was endorsed by the gig workers surveyed. As shown below, in response to the question, "Assume that you are looking for a new, additional gig. How important is being paid immediately for performance?," 83% of the gig workers stated it was very or somewhat important as a criterion when seeking out a new or additional gig.

Importance	Percentage Response
Very important	52%
Somewhat important	31%
Neither important nor unimportant	11%
Not important	4%
Not at all important	2%

Being paid immediately for performance was more important for female gig workers than for male gig workers, gig workers who were not married (as compared to those who were married), gig workers who had multiple gigs, and gig workers 35-54 years of age (compared to other gig workers). Such differences attest to the heterogeneity of the gig workforce.

- Relatedly, the amount of pay (compensation) was perceived as relatively important by the gig workers surveyed. When asked the question, "When looking for gig work, which, if any, of the following characteristics is *most important* to you?," a plurality, 29% of those surveyed, said that amount of compensation was most important, whereas 27% said flexibility of schedule was most important. Percentage responses to the question in the 2023 survey are displayed below for the total sample.

Characteristic Importance	Percentage Response
Amount of compensation	29%
Flexibility of schedule	27%
Personal interest in gig	19%
How frequently get paid	11%
Payment method	7%
Payment account security	4%
None are important	3%

Percentage response distributions for this question were relatively similar across sample subgroups, although female gig workers indicated that flexibility of schedule was slightly more important than did male gig workers; and multiple gig workers indicated that flexibility of schedule was slightly less important than did gig workers who only pursued a single gig.

Gig Worker Heterogeneity

The changes observed in the percentages of gig workers pursuing different gigs and gig categories are related to, or perhaps even driven by, the characteristics of individuals recently entering the gig economy. Simply stated, people entering the gig economy either during or post-COVID seem to differ from their pre-COVID counterparts on certain attributes. For example, as noted previously, whereas about one-quarter of the gig workers surveyed in 2020 performed professional services or freelance computer work (gigs that are often more than part-time and suggest a focus on only one gig), the corresponding percentage in 2023 was about 12%.

This decline in percentages is reflected in household income and educational levels. In 2020, approximately 34% of the gig workers surveyed reported that they had an annual household income in excess of $100,000, and 72% stated they possessed a post-high school education degree. In 2023, approximately 17% of the gig workers surveyed stated that they had an annual household income in excess of $100,000, and 42% stated they possessed a higher education degree. Such differences reflect the nature of gig work pre- and post-pandemic as well as the characteristics of the gig workers performing the work.

Similarly, the demographic composition of the gig workforce changed in other ways from 2020 to 2023. Consider the following comparisons:

- In 2020, 72% of the gig workers surveyed were white/Caucasian. In 2023, the figure was 66%.

- In 2020, 14% of the gig workers surveyed reported residing in a rural area. By 2023 that percentage had increased to 21%.

- In 2020, 69% of the gig workers surveyed owned their own homes. By 2023 that percentage had declined to 51%.

- In 2020, 54% of the gig workers surveyed said they were married. By 2023 that percentage had shrunk to 41%.

Even so, certain demographic characteristics remained fairly constant between 2020 and 2023. For example, the age distributions of gig workers in 2020 and 2023 were nearly identical, and the percentages of household income contributed by gig work in the two years were very similar.

Apart from a general desire to "earn more money," the gig workforce is not a homogeneous aggregate of individuals. Rather, as documented above, it consists of numerous subsets of individuals who share certain behaviors and motivations yet differ on other attributes. Consequently, any attempt to define or profile an "average" or "typical" gig worker is not likely to prove meaningful. To illustrate the heterogeneity existing in the gig workforce, two examples are considered. Both examples are relatively "high level." One is a comparison of male and female gig workers. The other is an overview of differences among gig workers of different ages.

Gender Differences

Comparisons of male and female gig workers surveyed in 2023 revealed that 37% of males had only one gig whereas 44% of females had only one gig. The most frequently reported gig for males was home repair (18%), whereas the most frequently reported gig for females was selling products or services they made themselves (17%). The same percentages of female and male gig workers (15%) participated in delivery services. Although the ages of the male and female gig workers were about the same, and even though the percentages of male and female gig workers who were married were virtually the same, male gig workers were less likely to have children under the age of 18 than were female gig workers.

The two inserts below show the expected and actual monthly gig income distributions for female and male gig workers who had only one gig or multiple (two or more) gigs in 2023.

Expected Gig Income Per Month	One Gig		Multiple Gigs	
	Females	**Males**	**Females**	**Males**
Less than $300	63%	46%	54%	40%
$300 to $499	15%	22%	17%	19%
$500 to $999	13%	14%	14%	17%
More than $1,000	9%	18%	15%	24%

Actual Gig Income Per Month	One Gig		Multiple Gigs	
	Females	**Males**	**Females**	**Males**
Less than $300	60%	48%	51%	39%
$300 to $499	16%	21%	17%	20%
$500 to $999	13%	15%	17%	16%
More than $1,000	11%	16%	15%	25%

These income distributions support five general inferences:

- Female gig workers expected to earn less from their gigs than did male gig workers.

- Female gig workers earned less from their gigs than did male gig workers.

- Both female and male gig workers earned about what they expected to earn from their gigs.

- Gig workers (both female and male) who had multiple gigs expected to earn more per month than gig workers who had only one gig.

- Gig workers (both female and male) who had multiple gigs earned more per month than gig workers who had only one gig.

Male and female gig workers who worked only one gig spent about the same amount of time on that gig. However, 60% of the female gig workers working only one gig reported earning less than $300 per month, compared with 48% of the males working only one gig. The difference may be due in part to the nature of the respective gigs worked as well as the length of time gig workers had worked their gigs; males exhibited a tendency to have worked their gigs longer than females. This difference is illustrated by when individuals started working their gigs and is especially manifest for gig workers pursuing more than one gig. Of the gig workers with multiple gigs, 62% of the females started working their gigs prior to the pandemic, whereas 71% of the males started working their gigs before the pandemic. Thus, the nature of the gigs worked together with length of experience working them may account for some of the differences in earnings. Regardless, the reasons for female-male earning differences are likely more complex than reported in the mass media.

Since the household income distributions of the male and female gig workers were similar, the difference in gig incomes for one-gig workers resulted in the finding that gig income was less than 10% of household income for 38% of the male gig workers, whereas it was less than 10% for 49% of female survey participants. Relatedly, female gig workers surveyed were slightly more likely to use their gig earnings to pay household bills than were male gig workers surveyed. For example, relatively more male gig workers (24%) than female gig workers (17%) working one gig were able to save or invest their gig earnings. Although the percentages differed, similar relationships were observed for primary and secondary gigs for the female and male gig workers surveyed. In brief, viewed across a variety of characteristics, it appears that both the motivations and behaviors of male and female gig workers were noticeably different.

Age Differences

Similarly, gig-related behaviors were observed to differ across age groups. The insert below illustrates the relative differences in behavior and motivations of gig workers in different age classifications. To facilitate comparisons across the age classifications, responses of individuals in the different age classifications were indexed relative to the total sample of gig workers. Across-age comparisons were made involving individuals who worked only one gig ("1 Gig"), individuals whose only or primary gig was delivery services ("Delivery Gig"), individuals who stated the primary reason they entered the gig economy was because they needed money ("Needed $"), and individuals who stated the primary use of their gig earnings was to pay household bills ("Pay HH Bills").

		Only/Primary		
Age Category	1 Gig	Delivery Gig	Needed $		Pay HH Bills
18-34	96	144	106	112	84
35-54	88	100	114	120	123
55+	126	56	32	67	103
Total Sample	100	100	100	100	100

The interpretation of the insert is as follows. The total sample was assigned to an index value of 100. Index numbers larger than 100 signify a higher percentage of the age category than found in the total sample. Consequently, relative to the total sample of gig workers and the other age categories, the major implications of the age insert are that:

• Gig workers 18-34 were more likely than others to pursue a delivery service gig because they needed money for reasons other than to pay household bills.

• Gig workers 35-54 were more likely than others to pursue multiple gigs because they had a greater need for money to pay household bills.

• Gig workers 55 years of age or older were more likely than others to pursue only one gig that was not a delivery gig, and they had a lesser need for money than other gig workers.

Key Takeaways

The research presented here illustrates the nuances and trends that exist in the gig economy and associated gig workforce in the United States. The gig economy is growing exponentially, more than four times faster than the traditional economy, and the number of individuals that engage in gig work is likewise increasing rapidly. As the research reported here documents, the structure of the gig workforce is evolving to accommodate new gig work opportunities and the desire of gig workers for flexibility and freedom. Notably, in the context of decision making, there is no "average" gig worker, and attempts at such a characterization are fruitless and likely to produce misleading inferences and poor decisions. The only commonality among gig workers is the need for "more money" (increasingly needed to pay household bills).

In particular:

- No specific gig activity category dominates the gig economy. For instance, fewer than 1-in-12 gig workers pursued a platform-based ride sharing gig activity in 2023, despite the extensive media coverage given to this activity and its frequent positioning as the prototypical gig activity.

- Similarly, online platform-based gig activities are only one segment of the gig economy, despite the fact that they are accorded to a majority of the media's attention.

- Female gig workers expect to earn less than male gig workers and actually do earn less. However, the reasons underlying the discrepancy are numerous, complex, and explainable.

- Perhaps contrary to the conclusion that there is no "average" gig worker, the gig workforce is trending toward being "average Americans" as more individuals enter the gig economy. (This inference is perhaps a tautology given the growing size of the gig workforce in the United States.)

• Likewise, perhaps contrary to the "need for more money," a considerable proportion of the gig workforce engages in gig work for reasons that are not strictly pecuniary.

• The nature and scope of gig opportunities are changing as a function of economic and societal changes as well as changes wrought by the pandemic. More individuals currently pursue multiple gigs than pursue only one gig.

• There is little distinction between a primary gig and a secondary gig among individuals who work multiple gigs in terms of the nature of the gigs pursued, the time spent on their gigs, or the earnings received from their gigs.

No doubt driven in part by the global pandemic, the changes occurring in the gig economy and the gig workforce require creative forward thinking for firms to remain competitive. For example, gig work is forcing changes for gig and non-gig companies alike in the traditional ways of paying for performance. To wit, 83% of the survey participants cited the importance of being paid quickly. This suggests that competitive advantages will accrue to those firms that pay through flexible options such as virtual cards, mobile wallets, and crypto currency.

It is imperative that firms understand and appreciate the heterogeneity that exists among gigs and gig workers, and how that heterogeneity can be embraced and leveraged for success. Thinking beyond the present research, the nature of work itself is likely to be redefined and refined by changes taking place in the gig economy. Non-gig-related firms are already considering internal gig marketplaces for one-off jobs, and educational institutions are readying training programs to fill the void created by the needs of independent contract workers. Gig-induced disruptions will be commonplace in the years and decades ahead.

Appendix E

To obtain empirical and objective insights into gig workers' behaviors and motivations, nationwide surveys of self-identified gig workers were conducted in July 2020 and April 2023. Given the nearly three-year gap between the two surveys, the surveys effectively bookended the pandemic, and differences in the results of the two surveys can be loosely attributed, at least in part, to the pandemic and consequent movement to work from home. This time-gap also allows inferences as to possible trends in the gig economy and insights as to what might constitute the gig economy as well as the gig workforce in the future.

The research design employed in both surveys was identical to permit comparisons and inferences across the time period. In general, the research methodology consisted of standard, accepted research techniques and procedures. Hence, the results should be valid and reliable within the research parameters and generalize to self-identified gig workers in the United States.

Both samples consisted of self-identified gig workers who were members of a large, 60 million-plus internet consumer panel (Dynata). In each survey, a random selection of panel members was invited to participate. Every panel member accepting the invitation to participate was asked a set of screening (qualifying) questions; those "passing" the screening questions were provided the following description of a gig ("side hustle" or part-time job):

> A **gig** is defined as a flexible work arrangement that allows a person to work how, when, and where he or she wants to work. Even full-time and part-time employees may sometimes work **gigs** in their free time.

Potential survey participants then read a list of illustrative gig activities and were asked whether they had worked a gig in the past 12 months. Individuals answering positively were asked how many different gigs they had worked in the past 12 months and then were shown a list of 14 different gig categories (plus an "other" category). Depending on how many gigs they reported working in the past 12 months, survey participants were asked about either their only gig or if they reported working more than one gig, about their primary and secondary gigs. Survey participants resided in 50 states and the District of Colombia. The geographical distribution of survey participants closely followed the distribution of state populations 18 years of age and older.

The questionnaires administered in the two surveys consisted of a set of common or "core" questions as well as unique questions. The focus of this report is primarily on responses to the common questions, with a secondary focus on selected question responses to the 2023 survey.

Ultimately, 1,001 gig workers constituted the 2020 sample, and 2,019 gig workers constituted the 2023 sample. In 2020, 51% of the sample consisted of males; in 2023 the corresponding percentage was 50%. In 2020, 35% of the samples were 18-34 years of age, 39% was 35-54 years of age, and 26% was 55 years of age or older. Corresponding age percentages for the 2023 sample were 36%, 37%, and 27%. Potential survey participants who did not answer the gender or age questions, or who were younger than 18 years of age, were excluded from participating. Because both surveys were cross-sectional in that they documented gig worker characteristics at a single point in time, causal inferences are not warranted.

Selected Question and Responses

	Only 1 Gig - 2023	Primary Gig - 2023	Secondary Gig - 2023	2021	2020
How have you been working your gig?	Percent	Percent	Percent		
I do not use digital tools	31.3%	23.4%	29.7%		
I use digital tools in conjunction with limited personal interaction with customers or clients	29.5%	30.3%	26.7%		
I use digital tools to connect with customers or clients, but my work is based on personal interaction	21.1%	32.5%	26.7%		
I only use digital tools with no personal interaction with customers or clients	18.1%	13.8%	16.9%		
When you started your gig, how much money did you expect to make?	Percent	Percent	Percent	Percent	Percent
Less than $100/month	30.6%	18.1%	25.4%	22.3%	22.9%
$100 − $299/month	24.1%	24.7%	25.4%	26.3%	24.9%
$300 - $499/month	18.6%	17.9%	18.3%	22.0%	18.6%
$500 - $999/month	13.0%	16.4%	14.2%	14.0%	14.1%
$1,000 - $1,999/month	7.5%	12.2%	9.4%	6.7%	9.5%
$2,000 - $2,999/month	2.6%	5.9%	3.5%	8.7%	10.0%
$3,000 - $3,999/month	1.3%	1.8%	1.7%		
More than $4,000/month	2.3%	3.0%	2.1%		
About how much time in a week do you spend working your gig?	Percent	Percent	Percent	Percent	Percent
Less than 4 hours a week	29.7%	20.9%	32.4%	24.0%	28.9%
4 to 8 hours a week	34.8%	33.7%	32.8%	46.6%	32.9%
1 to 3 days a week	20.5%	23.6%	22.6%	13.8%	18.2%
4 or more days a week	15.0%	21.8%	12.2%	15.6%	20.0%
How much do you earn from your gig?	Percent	Percent	Percent	Percent	Percent
Less than $100/month	28.1%	16.5%	25.5%	20.8%	20.0%
$100 − $299/month	26.3%	21.9%	24.7%	24.5%	26.6%
$300 - $499/month	18.1%	19.5%	18.5%	25.1%	17.8%
$500 - $999/month	14.1%	17.5%	15.0%	13.6%	15.3%
$1,000 - $1,999/month	7.8%	11.2%	9.7%	8.0%	10.5%
$2,000 - $2,999/month	2.2%	6.8%	3.6%	8.0%	9.8%
$3,000 - $3,999/month	1.2%	2.9%	1.3%		
More than $4,000/month	2.2%	3.7%	1.7%		
How do you primarily use the money you earn from your gig?	Percent	Percent	Percent	Percent	Percent
Pay household bills	49.6%	49.2%	45.2%	34.3%	36.9%
Save or invest	20.1%	20.7%	22.2%	24.1%	30.8%
Improve personal lifestyle	14.0%	15.4%	17.0%	16.5%	15.6%
Support needs of children	7.5%	8.7%	8.0%	9.5%	4.9%
Other (Please describe);	5.4%	3.1%	2.9%	2.3%	3.4%
Pay school expenses	2.0%	1.7%	2.8%	6.0%	4.0%
Charitable giving	1.4%	1.2%	1.9%	7.3%	4.4%

	Only 1 Gig - 2023	Primary Gig - 2023	Secondary Gig - 2023
How long have you been working your gig?	Percent	Percent	Percent
Less than 3 months	21.7%	14.5%	25.5%
3 - 6 Months	20.0%	23.4%	24.1%
7 - 11 months	13.7%	16.2%	15.5%
12 months or longer	44.6%	45.9%	34.9%
* Did you start working this gig...	Percent	Percent	Percent
before the COVID pandemic	70.1%	66.7%	66.8%
during the COVID pandemic	29.9%	33.3%	33.2%
Why did you take on your gig?	Percent	Percent	Percent
Needed more money	45.8%	43.7%	43.3%
Enjoy the work	18.8%	17.1%	18.4%
Had the available time to work	9.2%	9.2%	10.2%
Allowed me greater flexibility to decide when I wanted to work	8.7%	11.2%	7.3%
Allowed me to diversify my income streams	7.4%	9.4%	8.9%
To explore different interests or passions	6.9%	6.9%	6.3%
Hoping to make the secondary gig a primary gig	NA	NA	3.3%
Other (please specify):	3.2%	2.5%	2.3%
About how often do you get paid when working this gig?	Percent	Percent	Percent
Immediately upon finishing	38.8%	40.2%	42.2%
Every day	11.9%	11.3%	11.7%
Every 2 - 3 days	6.7%	9.4%	9.3%
Every 4 - 6 days	4.0%	3.9%	4.3%
Weekly	18.6%	18.7%	17.7%
Bi-weekly	9.2%	8.5%	7.2%
Monthly	10.8%	8.0%	7.6%
How are you paid when you work your gig?	Percent	Percent	Percent
Cash or check	40.6%	37.6%	39.7%
Direct bank deposit	35.0%	33.2%	30.2%
Mobile wallet, cash app, or the like	21.2%	25.9%	26.9%
Other (please specify):	2.3%	2.2%	1.9%
Crypto currency	0.9%	1.1%	1.3%

*Only asked survey participants working a gig 12 months or longer

Who pays you when working your gig?	Percent	Percent	Percent
I am paid directly by my customers or clients	46.4%	51.2%	51.8%
The company I work my gig with pays me	39.0%	37.3%	33.9%
I am paid by a third-party payment provider	11.8%	9.9%	11.2%
Do not know	2.8%	1.6%	3.1%

How do you primarily access the money you make from your gig?	Percent	Percent	Percent
Through transfer to personal bank account	37.5%	32.3%	32.0%
Via cash	24.6%	26.8%	26.2%
With a plastic debit card	20.5%	24.2%	24.4%
Via check	7.8%	5.4%	6.2%
With a virtual debit card	7.0%	9.0%	9.5%
Other (please specify)	2.6%	2.3%	1.7%
Please indicate what you most dislike about your gig.	**Percent**	**Percent**	**Percent**
No dislikes	36.6%	30.2%	33.6%
The pay rate	16.7%	16.0%	16.3%
The time necessary to complete the work	10.8%	9.5%	10.9%
The hours available to work	8.7%	10.7%	11.1%
Changing or unclear pay structure	5.8%	8.3%	5.1%
Interfering with family time	5.4%	6.2%	4.9%
Other (please specify):	4.5%	3.7%	2.6%
Lack of job satisfaction	4.0%	3.9%	3.9%
The time it takes to be paid	3.9%	5.8%	6.9%
Poor work-life balance	3.6%	5.7%	4.7%

Note: There was one exception in the 2023 survey. The representation of gig workers in only one state, California, in the sample differed percentagewise from the adult population in that state. California represents 7.6% of the sample but comprises 11.7% of the United States population 18 years of age and older. The under-representation of gig workers from California in the sample might be a consequence of California's Assembly Bill 5, which restricted opportunities for gig workers.

MORE THAN A TEMPORARY PHENOMENON
Myths and Implications

The continuous growth and appeal of gig work is not a trend or fad, but more of a revolution in how work can be accomplished, an alternative way to engage the workforce. Flexibility in how work can be done has now evolved to a few thousand choices which are subsets of the 4 major categories of gig workers identified in *Ultimate Gig* which were: Transportation Gigs, Service Gigs, Selling Gigs, and Leasing Gigs. Gig providing companies are fulfilling a new need, perhaps a new demand by the marketplace of workers.

Myth #1. Gig Workers are Homogeneous. **Fact:** Gig Workers are Heterogeneous. There is no meaningful "average gig worker."

The gig workforce is very heterogeneous, both in terms of behaviors and motivations, and not recognizing differences can lead to poor decision making by companies and public officials alike...

Myth #2. Gig Workers are primarily Uber, Lyft, Door Dash Drivers. **Fact:** Transportation and Delivery Services represent a significant segment of gig workers. However, the gig economy is much broader than platform-based ridesharing or delivery services, even though they currently seem to draw the most media attention. Likewise, gigs based solely on the use of digital tools, or the internet are a relatively small proportion of all gigs...

Myth #3: Gig workers engage in gigs for immediate extra money. **Fact:** Gig workers are intentional about their earnings. Although the primary reason people enter the gig economy is to earn more money, a substantial proportion of gig workers indicated a non-monetary reason drove their entry into the gig economy, reinforcing the conclusion of a heterogeneous gig workforce.

An important—and perhaps surprising—finding of the research was that half of the gig workers surveyed said they were paid either immediately upon finishing a gig (40%) or paid every day (12%). When combined with the finding that 83% of the gig workers surveyed said that it was very important or important to be paid immediately when looking for a new, additional gig, the findings suggest new, innovative means of payment may well be a competitive advantage for companies that can leverage this desire.

Despite the fact that there is no average gig worker, over time the gig workforce is beginning to increasingly resemble the "mainstream American workforce."

Implications

The current discussions relative to how independent contractors will be defined will probably span several years before consensus is gained among all stakeholders including public policy makers, firms, and the workers who choose to work as an independent contractor – the gig worker.

We are experiencing, in mature markets throughout the world, a growing number of people desirous of flexible work opportunities who are choosing to work as a micro entrepreneur or independent contractor. This trend is expected to result in over 50% of the workforce being involved in gig work in a few years. Approximately 40% of the workforce is currently involved.

Conversations are also emerging relative to independent contractor classification, especially among public policy makers. Many business models are challenged by the possibility that independent contractors would be classified as employees because some think that firms who utilize independent contractors are abusing the worker by not providing the worker with benefits similar to those of an employee. However, the underlying conversation may be more about ensuring that income taxes are paid, and regulations adhered to, more so than whether workers receive benefits or not when they choose to be an independent contractor.

New Safety Nets are available.....We predict that safety net products, insurance and basic guidance for the independent contractor designed to support their ability to maximize their potential will become available and affordable.

Workers choose to be independent contractors for important reasons. They seek flexibility and freedom in how the work can be accomplished, and they do not want to be held to the rigidity of traditional work hours. Often, the workers who choose to be independent contractors cannot work traditional hours or they are choosing to be their own boss and work when and how they choose. Freedom of choice is an uncommon freedom and certainly a precious freedom. All involved in attempting to define an independent contractor should always be aware of the fact that, in this country, freedom is a very important component of the fabric of our free enterprise system.

The gig economy is growing. This new phenomenon which attracts people from all walks of life to flexible work opportunities is not new. We do not identify the pandemic as being responsible for the major shift from traditional work to more flexible work opportunities. The pandemic simply accelerated the transformation from a more industrialized economy to one which thrives on flexibility vs rigidity and innovative technology which enables us to accomplish more with less. The needs associated with family life or caring for someone near and dear may prevent working at specific times on specific days. The vast majority of those who work in the gig economy as independent contractors are striving to convert underutilized time and/or assets into income earning opportunities. The vast majority are not seeking to replace full time work with their gig. Some are seeking to replicate or create a full-time income earning opportunity based upon micro enterprise principles, however, this segment of gig worker represents only 10% of those involved ... Welcome to the *NEW ECONOMY*!

LOOKING AT THE FUTURE OF THE GIG ECONOMY
Robert A. Peterson, PhD

It well may take several years, even decades, before gig workers and microentrepreneurs themselves, companies large and small and their customers, public policymakers, and the general public fully understand and appreciate the business model implications of the *NEW ECONOMY* and its underlying entrepreneurial agency that has created a major societal and cultural shift in the way business is conducted. While the gig economy is projected to grow at a double-digit rate in the near future, as the number of gig workers continue to grow, that growth is likely to be less than the annual 16%+ observed in recent years. This is so for several reasons, including the number of people who want to be gig workers and the number of gig possibilities. What are the gigs that individuals will pursue in both the short term and the long term? Many of the gigs that will need to exist in the future probably do not exist today. How will the gig workforce evolve given the incursion of AL and bots, human needs that are currently unknown, and the increasing number of people seeking to be gig workers? Who thought about mobile dog grooming on a large scale just a decade ago? The gig economy will evolve into the *NEW ECONOMY* in a form or fashion presently unknown, but faster that we realize.

By peering into the future just a bit, several implications and consequences of the *NEW ECONOMY* are visible. For example, regardless of its structure or even size in the future, the gig economy will likely continue to change the manner in which work is performed. The principle of pay-for-performance (especially for on-demand work) will be incorporated into workplaces and strategic plans of all ilk. This will be a cultural change. Organizations will have to evaluate the tradition of people working 9am to 5pm versus simply accomplishing assigned work tasks and being paid for same. AI-based scheduling platforms will be created to manage sizable gig workforces. Unions will have to rethink their purpose, both with respect to the pay-for-performance principle and worker representation. For unions, the issue is whether they become stronger—to represent groups of gig microentrepreneurs—or weaker—if gig microentrepreneurs do not want or need to pay dues to something providing questionable benefits.

As the gig economy includes more and more gig microentrepreneurs while old gigs disappear and new gigs are created or simply evolve, there will be an increasing need to train (gig) workers. Since, by definition, gig microentrepreneurs are independent contractors not beholden to a particular hiring entity, the issue will arise regarding who in the *NEW ECONOMY* will do the training, and who will pay for the training required for specialized skills. Companies will be reluctant to train someone who might be working for a competitor, either concurrently or tomorrow. Such training might be conducted by new types of organizations, both nonprofit and for-profit, and often online.

The new breed of gig entrepreneur will likely have lasting impact on our thinking about entrepreneurial education. Universities and colleges, especially public regional colleges and community colleges, are likely to bear the brunt of providing training for a broad range of activities and skills that can be applied across a diverse range of income-producing tasks, especially those related to the application of artificial intelligence-based tools. This will create a need for instructors who can teach these activities and skills, which will in turn lead to a new category of gig workers.

The question of organizational loyalty will need to be addressed in the *NEW ECONOMY* since, by definition and unless curtailed by regulation, gig microentrepreneurs could potentially work for competitors on succeeding days or simply refuse to work on certain days when the need for freedom and flexibility overwhelms the need for income. What incentives must organizations offer to attract and retain a predictable and stable independent workforce, one that might be exposed to its intimate strategic, tactical, and even financial secrets? What constraints will need to be imposed and balanced with information required for successfully completing work-related tasks?

One intriguing attribute of the *NEW ECONOMY* is already being employed in some firms. Firms that occasionally need specialists for a specific project or just additional short-term workers due to their business cycle could learn from the gig economy by creating "internal talent platforms." Firms employing internal talent platforms facilitate their own employees taking on "extra work" for "extra money"—the basic premise of the gig economy. Thus, rather than bringing in consultants or hiring short-term employees or independent contractors to respond to specific needs, firms might encourage their own employees to "bid" on internal project tasks using gig economy principles. Not only would this allow employees to earn incremental remuneration, it would also harness expertise and talent that already exists within the firm, permit employees to experience different aspects of the firm, perhaps increase firm loyalty, minimize costs of attracting outside workers, and protect the firm's intellectual property by keeping activities in-house. This is just one example of a potential positive externality reflective of the gig economy, and why the *NEW ECONOMY* will have a cultural impact.

A standard criticism of the general concept of the gig economy is that gig microentrepreneurs do not receive benefits accruing to company employees, such as health insurance, paid vacations, or retirement plans. As the number of gig microentrepreneurs increases, capitalism will likely ensure that there will be organizations and platforms created that provide safety-net products and services that serve the needs of groups of basically unrelated individuals. These organizations or platforms may arise from existing organizations, or they may result from innovations that are currently unforeseen or non-existent. The Association for Entrepreneurship is a prime example of a private sector organization successfully offering safety-net services for (unrelated) gig workers.

In sum, although it is always risky to try to predict the future, gig microentrepreneurs, companies, consumers, and government agencies will all benefit from the growth in the gig economy. The vast array of gig activities in which gig microentrepreneurs engage clearly shows the need for an on-demand workforce. There are both economic and societal benefits to having a labor force that can conduct a wide range of tasks with varying timeframes. Whether gig microentrepreneurs are engaging in gig work to augment their income because of economic insecurity or for intrinsic reasons, the motivations, and behaviors of gig microentrepreneurs are indicative of the talent and resources needed to keep the U.S. economy moving forward positively.

Perspective #1. Insights and Outlook

Every segment in our society has options and choices that were not available just a few years ago. The stats and facts suggest that traditional income earning opportunities for the average worker will not keep pace with inflation. Ironically, this fact is not new. It is important to note that while inflation may be record-breaking, there have been significant trends that have been emerging long before the recent price increases on products and services that we are now experiencing here in the United States.

The primary challenge facing the average person, based upon the stats and facts presented, is the need to balance the profit and loss statement. For individuals, the more practical terminology would be: **Ensure that we earn more than we spend and manage the difference prudently and wisely.** Providing insight on how we ensure that the previous statement is the reality of our individual lives is one of the primary objectives of this book.

Challenges that individuals cannot control are often imposed or created by external forces such as corporations, organizations, and governance. Public policy makers control much of what governments will do to protect the health of the communities and societies in which we live. Challenges are also created as a result of innovation that triggers change. For every challenge, there will be a response. The response can be defensive of a traditional norm, or the response can be additional fuel for innovation and its positive impact on changes to the norms we have been traditionally accustomed to. The current growth in entrepreneurial activities in combination with the desire for more simplicity, flexibility, and freedom of choice in how work can be done has changed the way we work. Therefore, traditional norms such as the way we pay taxes and seek benefits traditionally managed and offered by the employer model, is now questioned by some public policy makers in an attempt to keep certain traditional norms in place vs complete adoption of a new way to work. An example of the preceding statement would be the challenge consistently faced by companies that utilize intermediaries/independent contractors in their channels of distribution. The independent contractor does not rely on specific wages for specific hours of work. Compensation is based solely upon performance. Such a concept enables efficiencies in how work is done. These efficiencies are real and benefit both the provider of the work opportunity and the worker. The independent contractor basically determines the value of the time they invest by striving to execute the work in a successful manner. There are no wage guarantees. The trade-off is accepted because flexibility and freedom of choice are gained.

The **average amount saved by Americans has decreased** compared to prior years. In January 2025, Americans saved **4.6% of their disposable income**, down from **5.3%** a decade earlier. This is significantly lower than the peak savings rate of **33.7%** during the COVID-19 pandemic

Before COVID-19, it can be said that while average incomes had been growing overall, the appeal of part-time work opportunities and the attribute of flexibility had been growing as well, fueling the growth of the gig economy. COVID-19 revealed how vulnerable we can become from a health and well-being perspective and an economic perspective. COVID-19 has also revealed our dependency on traditional labor and exposed the inefficiencies associated with many concepts learned during the industrial revolution. Those forced to work from home have remained productive and may have an even greater desire to find work that allows the ability to continue to work on a flexible schedule.

The perceived need to organize work from fixed facilities with fixed expenses has been changing. New thinking has accelerated. The financial stress of rent, mortgage, and associated expenses in operating a facility will not be a priority for all types of labor providers. We continue to witness office building vacancies and shopping mall traffic that is a fraction of years past.

More employers are expected to explore and provide more flexible work opportunities creating a more efficient business model for the business and adding more choices to gig work possibilities. The use of independent contractors, we predict, will grow even faster than prior growth rates relative to the gig economy. This is not a new conversation; COVID 19 has simply accelerated what we have been experiencing for years.

In July 2017, Deloitte Consulting featured an article titled "The Future of Work" in their Deloitte Review. John Hagel, Jeff Schwartz, and Josh Bersin authored the article. This article provided us with a detailed glimpse of what work might look like in the future. We were advised in that article the following:

> "Businesses must prepare to redesign work and jobs to take advantage of the growing capabilities of machines and the need to retrain and redeploy people to higher-value and more productive and engaging jobs working alongside smart machines and many types of workers—on and off the balance sheet, in crowds, and around the world." In that article, the authors went on to provide us with more of a glimpse as to where we are headed: "Public institutions will be wise to proactively prepare for educational challenges, including support for new types of work and workers and a more entrepreneurial economy."

Our reality: We are experiencing what others foresaw many years ago. The economic stress of change, shrinking jobs, a movement away from nine to five traditional work hours, new forms of work, and the growing appeal of flexibility in virtually everything we are involved, is real. Another financial reality worth noting is the fact that while wages have increased significantly over the past 40 years, inflation has caused our purchasing power to remain relatively flat. We may be earning more, on average, as individuals, however, we may not be able to buy much more with the dollars we spend. When we dig into the data, it is easy to see why many Americans, and their counterparts in mature markets around the world, are looking for ways to earn income beyond their traditional jobs. This concern has been brewing and maturing over the past decade. Economic pressures are real.

From this perspective, we are moving more toward an economy more inclusive versus being exclusive to the smaller percentage who currently control much of the wealth. The preceding statement and perception depend on personal insights and decisions. The *NEW ECONOMY*, from our perspective, is more inclusive. The possibilities associated with entrepreneurial activities who adopt the mindset of the architect have never been greater!

Perspective #2. Freelance Work

In 2021, 52% of workers who planned to quit their job admit that they were considering a freelance career instead. The gig economy has grown faster than the traditional job market. Approximately 50% of all businesses hire freelancers.

Freelancing has become the most popular form of gig work contrary to many perceptions that tend to lean toward thinking that transportation gigs are the only form of gig. Freelancing enables the leverage of non-tangible assets in the form of time, knowledge, skills, and experience. Medical doctors, attorneys and accountants, educators/teachers, consultants in a variety of formats, technologists, graphic artists, writers, are all found in the ranks of freelancers.

New platform-based companies that pioneered the ability, through technology, to connect talent with those who need talent on more of a temporary basis vs full time employment have made freelancing a viable option for activating the concept of leverage.

The **largest connector of freelancers with employers** is **Freelancer.com**, which has an estimated **60+ million employers and freelancers** on the platform. Another significant platform is **Upwork**, which has around **18 million users**.

Freelancers earn well. Over 10,000 skills are connected by platforms such as Upwork and Freelancer and there are many more. Over 30% of Fortune 100 companies have used Upwork, to identify and engage talent through a process that averages 3 days.

In **2024**, freelancers in the United States earned a median income of **$85,000**, surpassing full-time employees who earned around **$80,000**. Approximately **one in five freelancers** reported earning **$100,000 or more** annually, indicating a significant portion of freelancers are achieving substantial financial success

Businesses, large brands and small, find freelancing a viable choice for sourcing work because they can review work samples and experience quickly. The entire process happens online, and the employer of the freelancer only pays for performance. The process has proven to be safe and secure as Upwork boasts a client satisfaction rating of 4.9 out of 5.0 on its website.

Hayden Brown, President & CEO of Upwork, states on its website:

> *"Our mission to create economic opportunities so people have better lives has taken us so much further. As a result, we've become the world's work marketplace where everyday businesses of all sizes and independent talent from around the globe meet here to accomplish incredible things."*

Affiliate Marketing Opportunities have become popular. Many major brands now engage affiliate marketers often referred to as Influencers. These intermediaries are paid for influencing others who may shop the brand. Amazon, Walmart, and brands you may never have expected are offering affiliate marketing opportunities. Social media platforms, blogs, newsletters, personal websites and replicated websites of the brand enable affiliate marketers to promote the brand through their natural social networks. When customers make a purchase as a result of the influence/sharing/promotion, affiliates earn a commission. Some affiliates actually engage full time in these efforts. The income potential depends on success in promotion effectiveness. Some affiliates of major brands such as Amazon are known to have developed significant income potential from their engagement of this possibility.

Affiliate marketing opportunities are generally easy to understand, easy to engage and fun to leverage when you love the brand having been a satisfied customer. If you are passionate about a product, service or brand and you advocate your passion by recommending the product, service or brand to others, chances are you can engage in an affiliate marketing possibility.

Individual Entrepreneurship/Microenterprise Possibilities. Becoming an entrepreneur has traditionally required a willingness to assume risk, often substantial risk, in exchange for the opportunity to be in total control of a work opportunity and the possibility of fair rewards. The entrepreneurial story, foundational to the American story, and the attributes of free enterprise, have always enabled exciting possibilities. Ordinary people have accomplished extraordinary outcomes, building small and big businesses, some of which have become recognizable brands.

Entrepreneurs create an enterprise which serves a need. When the need is fulfilled, the enterprise profits and so do the many people involved in the process. Employees benefit from the activities created by the enterprise. Most interesting is the fact that 89% of the total number of businesses in the US are classified as micro-businesses.

A micro-enterprise is typically defined as a small business with fewer than ten employees and a modest turnover. These businesses often require minimal startup capital, making them accessible for many individuals looking to start their own ventures. Micro-enterprises can include a variety of business types, such as local shops, service providers, and online businesses.

The new "microentrepreneur" is more of an aggregator of income streams. The microentrepreneur is not dependent on any one particular income stream. The aggregation and success of the microenterprise may not have any physical attribute. The microentrepreneur may not have any employees.

The microenterprise is a collection of opportunities executed well because Simplicity, Flexibility, Freedom of Choice, and the Gig Economy now make such an idea possible. As we shared earlier in this book, 69% of gig workers were found to be working multiple gigs based upon our research. This stat indicates the growing awareness of how multiple sources of income can be leveraged. Opportunities to work in accordance with personal preferences are more numerous. We are no longer limited to a sole source of income. An individual's ability to increase his or her income potential is only limited by the person's objectives, motivations, and the number of hours available to embrace a new activity. We are witnessing the emergence of the microentrepreneur who we also refer to as the Independent Entrepreneur or Solopreneur.

Direct Selling represents a very unique possibility and opportunity. The assertion in the title of this section is inferred but not stated in the book, *Ultimate Gig*. Over the past 3 years, as a result of more research, observation, and study, we have more insights to share. I, as author and members of the project team, have extensive experience gained over many years of direct and indirect involvement with the direct selling model. The direct selling model has been around in excess of 125 years founded on principles and values first utilized by companies such as Vorwerk, Avon and Stanley Home Products.

In the United States, direct selling companies utilize more than 6 million independent contractors to manage the primary responsibility of acquiring, selling, serving customers, and utilizing the influence of the already engaged independent contractor to attract others who are also interested in promoting the brand to attract and retain more customers. Direct selling supports flexibility in how the work is done and the ability to aggregate successful effort into the possibility of residual income possibilities resulting from customers and brand partners who continue to influence customer purchases directly and indirectly.

The direct selling company generally offers a very high-quality product, marketing support, and all of the coaching and training needed in a simple format, often a digital based tool or program. Therefore the learning required is easily accessed. For some direct sellers, the gig can turn into more of an entrepreneurial opportunity.

The direct seller who contributes to fostering a relationship with customers increases the likelihood of repurchase. This activates the possibility of a continuous and growing income stream as the direct seller influences more and more customers, directly and indirectly, to purchase over a period of time. When direct sellers are eligible to share such opportunities with others who do the same thing, the income possibility continues to increase through another dimension that has been activated. Because technology is the new enabler, direct sellers can market to others without geographic or time constraints.

The role of the direct seller is actually extraordinary because it is very similar to the role an agent or franchisee plays in the distribution channel of real estate brands, automobile brands, or fast-food brands. All distribution channels are focused on customer acquisition. In the other distribution models used as examples, intermediaries actually acquire the opportunity to engage customers through agencies, dealerships, and stores which usually require a very significant investment and high degree of skill.

The company utilizing a direct selling model as its primary channel of distribution accomplishes the same thing as an agency, dealership, franchise, or store. The difference: Direct selling companies utilize intermediaries in the form of people who can be from any walk of life, live in different geographies, and work with flexibility and freedom relative to how the work is accomplished. The investment required of a direct seller is low, usually minimal. The knowledge, skill, and experience required can be easily learned because the focus is more on sharing what you enjoy and love vs the more formal and sophisticated selling process of an agency, store or store related franchise.

A direct seller developing 12 to 24 customers will probably experience gig type income depending upon the average monthly purchase of those customers who continue to buy. Unlike most gig income, direct sellers can earn on the residual purchase of these customers when the direct sellers continue to meet the requirements their company may establish. Over time, consistent successful customer acquisition and retention becomes foundational to a consistent growing income possibility. Chapter 7 will explore Direct Selling Opportunities in more detail.

Perspective # 3.
FLEXIBILITY—FREEDOM—REWARDS

The mindset shared throughout the original Ultimate Gig Project Team, at the beginning of our exploration of the gig economy (2017), was very different at the beginning of the project vs what the collective mindset evolved to as the project matured.

The pandemic (2021 – 2023) certainly triggered an interest in flexible and alternative income possibilities. However, I like many others, embraced the idea that the gig economy was simply another form of part-time work. Part-time work was always engaged for the sole objective to engage an opportunity to earn part-time income during specific times such as after regular working hours or, for students, after school. These early assumptions were very problematic. In fact, they were very wrong. Fortunately, due to the rigor brought to our group by academic friends, we explored stats, facts, and conducted our own survey's which were always led by Robert A. Perterson, University of Texas, Austin Texas.

My thoughts and mindset changed rapidly as a result of study. I was more interested in new marketplace trends and behaviors vs traditional assumptions and personal experience which was now historical. Mentally, I did not want to be a personal version of Kodak or Block Buster, well recognized brands that did not embrace an understanding of the changes in marketplace behaviors that were about to impact their business models. I too, realized that I was a business model.

Whereas it is very easy to assume that money alone, or the opportunity to earn money quickly, might be the primary reason people from all walks of life were embracing the new gig economy possibilities, we found something very different. Early research indicated that there were multiple reasons why so many were attracted to the gig economy. *Hyperwallet,* a company that provided merchant processing services to direct selling companies (Hyperwallet later merged into PayPal) was one of the first to pay attention to the gig economy phenomenon. McKenzie Consulting, Deloitte, and others were also paying attention and started to write about *The Future Of Work.* Below is a direct lift from a quick online search about the Hyperwallet study conducted in 2017:

> *Hyperwallet's research on the gig economy reveals a significant shift in workforce dynamics, with a growing number of workers opting for gig jobs instead of traditional full-time positions. The study highlights the importance of payment speed, with over 77% of gig workers indicating they would prefer to work more gig work if they could receive their payments faster. Additionally, younger workers are more likely to embrace gig jobs compared to older generations. Hyperwallet's findings underscore the need for businesses to adjust their employee recruitment and retention strategies to meet the demands of the modern workforce. www.bing.com*

We soon realized that the gig economy was about so much more than we had thought. The chart which follows, which we attribute to Hyperwallet, McKenzie and Deloitte, provided us with insights that changed our mindsets immediately.

Top reasons Americans would leave their job to work in the gig economy

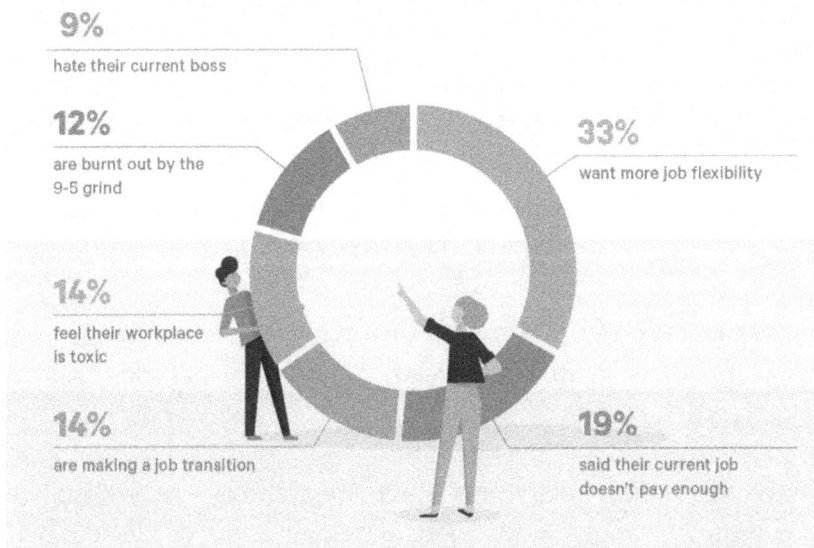

9%
hate their current boss

12%
are burnt out by the
9-5 grind

33%
want more job flexibility

14%
feel their workplace
is toxic

14%
are making a job transition

19%
said their current job
doesn't pay enough

As you can see in the chart above, first published around 2020, workers started to gravitate toward the gig economy for multiple reasons. The attributed of flexibility has always been the leader in any poll that we have reviewed. However, many leave traditional work because they are burnt out (12%), others because the work environment is toxic (14%), a significant percentage are in transition (14%) and 19% reported that their job simply does not pay enough.

As a result of continuous study of the gig economy, we chose to briefly promote our findings through the use of a "tagline." This is the logic behind the use of our tagline: **FLEXIBILITY – FREEDOM – REWARDS**, which was the tagline for *Ultimate Gig*, our first book and remains the tagline for ***NEW ECONOMY.***

FLEXIBILITY is chosen as the first word because this attribute has always topped anyone's survey of what motivates gig workers. **FREEDOM** is chosen as the second word because independent gig workers are also exercising an uncommon freedom to work when they desire, and often, as much or as little as they desire. The freedom to choose is special. **REWARDS** is the last word chosen because the money, as important as it is, was never found to be the sole or even the most important reason for embracing a gig. Therefore, this perspective deserves attention. We work for a "return on our work effort," and we expect fair rewards. Do not overlook the values and attributes of **FLEXIBILITY** and **FREEDOM** which enable fair **REWARDS.** It is because of the first two words, along with the third word in our tagline, that we hypothesize: Flexibility, Freedom & Fair Rewards are the key drivers of gig economy growth and the fuel now driving the *NEW ECONOMY.*

Perspective #4. - The Great Reset
How the NEW ECONOMY is Redefining Entrepreneurship
By W. Mark Bennett, Esq.

For most of the twentieth century, the story of work was predictable. You went to school, landed a job, and if you kept your head down and worked hard, you were rewarded with promotions, benefits, and eventually retirement. That was the bargain. But today, it's clear that bargain has expired.

Baby Boomers and Generation X - the cohorts who built their lives around that contract - are slowing down. Many have no interest in grinding out another decade the way they once did. Meanwhile, Millennials and Gen Z look at the sacrifices their parents made and simply say, *"No thanks."* For them, flexibility, meaning, and freedom aren't perks. They're non-negotiables. Deloitte's 2024 Global survey found that nearly half of Gen Z and over 60% of Millennials plan to leave their jobs within two years if they don't align with their values or lifestyle (Deloitte, 2024).

This generational clash would be disruptive enough on its own. But layered on top of it is artificial intelligence. AI is not just another tool; it's a seismic force already eliminating jobs once thought untouchable. Goldman Sachs estimates that as many as 300 million full-time jobs worldwide could be automated in the coming decade (Goldman Sachs, 2023). Legal research, copywriting, diagnostics, even elements of creative design, roles long thought to be safe, are now being transformed or replaced by algorithms.

At the same time, AI is lowering the barriers to entrepreneurship. Tasks that once required a team, graphic design, marketing campaigns, and customer support, can now be managed by a single entrepreneur with a laptop and the right software. McKinsey projects that generative AI could add up to 0.6 percentage points to global productivity growth annually through 2040, provided businesses and individuals adapt effectively (McKinsey, 2023).

So what happens when older generations step back, younger ones refuse to play by the old rules, and AI rewrites the game altogether? The answer is entrepreneurship. Not in the narrow sense of building a Fortune 500 company, but in the broad, everyday sense: people finding new ways to turn skills, passions, and creativity into income streams.

You see it everywhere. A hobbyist turns a craft into an Etsy shop. A teacher builds a TikTok following and monetizes it through brand deals. Freelancers from Lagos to Los Angeles use Upwork to sell skills across borders. In 2023, 64 million Americans, 38% of the workforce, freelanced in some capacity (Upwork, 2023). Pew Research reports that roughly one in six Americans have earned income from gig platforms, whether driving for Uber, delivering groceries, or managing tasks online (Pew Research Center, 2021).

The creator economy alone is booming. Valued at over $200 billion in 2024, it's expected to surpass a trillion by the early 2030s (Grand View Research, 2024). With little more than a smartphone, people are building audiences, monetizing expertise, and creating careers that didn't exist a decade ago. Entrepreneurship, in this sense, isn't just accessible, it's inevitable.

It's worth pausing to remember how different this is from just 10 or 20 years ago. Starting a business once meant filing paperwork, securing capital, leasing space, and waiting months, or even years, to test an idea. Today, anyone can spin up a Shopify storefront in an afternoon, run ads for a few dollars, and see results in days. AI will even draft the ad copy, design the logo, and analyze customer feedback. The time and cost required to experiment have collapsed, and with them, the risks that once kept people from trying.

Where does this leave traditional models of entrepreneurship? Historically, direct selling had a monopoly on the so-called "kitchen table entrepreneur." It offered stay-at-home parents or part-timers a way to bring in a second stream of income. But today, it competes with gig work, creator platforms, and online marketplaces that feel easier, safer, and more modern.

Looking ahead, the next five to ten years are going to be fascinating. Expect a mass influx of people trying entrepreneurship, driven partly by necessity as AI reshapes traditional work. Expect more "hybrid" identities - people who are part employee, part entrepreneur. Expect governments to scramble to catch up with how to regulate benefits, taxes, and worker protections in a world dominated by 1099 income. Expect companies that adapt quickly, whether they're gig platforms, e-commerce providers, direct sellers, affiliates, or agents, to be the big winners … winning the loyalty of this new class of entrepreneurs.

What makes this moment so unique isn't just the technology or the generational divide. It's the cultural expectation that work should mean more. A job is no longer just a paycheck; it's an extension of identity. That's why entrepreneurship resonates so strongly. It allows people to align income with passion, to turn hobbies into livelihoods, to create businesses that reflect who they are.

We are, in many ways, standing at the threshold of a once-in-a-generation reset and witnessing the most democratized wave of entrepreneurship in history. The tools are cheap, the platforms are global, and the desire for autonomy is universal. The *NEW ECONOMY* isn't a future possibility, it's here. For individuals, the challenge is to embrace entrepreneurship as both necessity and opportunity. For organizations, the challenge is to adapt or risk irrelevance.

Technology can create tools, but it cannot create connections. Companies that embrace transparency, compliance, and digital simplicity will not just survive this reset, they will lead it.

References

Deloitte. (2024, June 3). Deloitte Global 2024 Gen Z and Millennial Survey. https://www.deloitte.com/us/en/insights/topics/talent/deloitte-gen-z-millennial-survey.html

Goldman Sachs. (2023, April 5). Generative AI could raise global GDP by 7%. https://www.goldmansachs.com/insights/articles/generative-ai-could-raise-global-gdp-by-7-percent

McKinsey & Company. (2023, June 14). The economic potential of generative AI: The next productivity frontier. https://www.mckinsey.com/capabilities/mckinsey-digital/our-insights/the-economic-potential-of-generative-ai-the-next-productivity-frontier

Upwork. (2023, December 12). Freelance Forward 2023. https://www.upwork.com/research/freelance-forward-2023-research-report

Pew Research Center. (2021, December 8). The state of gig work in 2021. https://www.pewresearch.org/internet/2021/12/08/the-state-of-gig-work-in-2021/

Grand View Research. (2024). Creator Economy Market Size, Share, & Trends, 2024–2033. https://www.grandviewresearch.com/industry-analysis/creator-economy-market-report

CHAPTER 4
OPTIONS, CHOICES, EQUALIZERS

While the *NEW ECONOMY* represents new possibilities, the individual remains responsible for taking the responsibility to study and explore. The evidence is clear; more people than ever before are searching for options that enable an ability to increase income with the flexibility and freedom needed to maintain core responsibilities without the experience of disruption. We offer the following as guidance for both the seeker of possibilities and those who are already into their exploration of *NEW ECONOMY* possibilities.

1. **Optimize The Challenges.** A substantial segment of Americans are not doing as well as they may appear. Our recap of the financial data associated with workers in all major segments merely highlights the current situation with a simple purpose to inform, educate, and inspire. A study of the data we

provide is all one needs to realize that it is time to take control of one's own destiny.

When household income and wealth accumulation is minimized, it will impact all family members. This reality is true in all mature societies. Hoping that something will change to support the innate personal desire to live well and provide for family, has not proven to be a solution to the experience associated with the negative experiences of not being able to balance a budget, save and invest more. The evidence is clear; the "hope program" has not proven to be effective so why select this choice?

Ironically, the major challenges revealed in our review of the stats and facts are not new. There have been challenges for many years, even decades. Primary challenges remain in the financial areas of life. We do not look to identify average earnings by age group. As you have noted, we do track average savings. The average amount of savings/investments could be key indicators which correlate with happiness and satisfaction.

The Great Resignation of 2021 is also described as a challenge. It was unexpected to the degree it happened. The quit rate amongst traditional jobs in all regions within the United States hit an all-time high. Did people quit their jobs because they no longer wanted to work, or did they quit because their work was not satisfying? Did workers quit traditional jobs because the traditional approach to work no longer fit their shift in personal values? Was the pandemic a cause for the acceleration in traditional job quit rates? The answers to the questions will be the focus of research, surveys, and studies over the next few years.

We might agree that there are challenges. For businesses in particular, the same strategies and models are no longer as effective as they once were. There are also new innovations and new ways to do just about everything. There are also new

EQUALIZERS. Challenges are not always resolved by the collective body, be it organization, corporation, or the collective of public policy makers. Challenges can be overcome when individuals take control of their personal decision making and resolve to treat challenges as opportunities to learn more or do something differently.

The primary challenge facing the average person, based upon the stats and facts presented earlier, is the need to balance the profit and loss statement. For individuals, the more practical terminology would be: **Ensure that we earn more than we spend, manage, and invest the difference prudently and wisely.** Providing insight on how we ensure that the previous statement is the reality of our lives is the objective of this book. There are EQUALIZERS.

2. **Explore Your Options Carefully.** The choices have never been greater to engage and activate new and complementary income possibilities. The gig economy has provided easy to engage, easy to understand, opportunities. Because the gig economy utilizes technology in its many formats effectively, you can actually work some gigs whenever you desire be it 10 am or 10 pm and you always determine how much effort you are willing to invest.

3. **Activate EQUALIZERS.** Gig seekers can actually be engaged and working their new gig within a couple of days, often within hours. Pay is prompt upon completion of the work and always performance based. Traditions associated with the traditional work model which requires specific commitments of time and a specific location where the work must be done remain important. However, there are options for those who may think differently.

Deciding to complement traditional income appears to be smart. Developing multiple income streams, from this perspective, is thought to be very smart!

NEW ECONOMY EQUALIZERS

"Dedicated to all workers in all formats, all age groups, professional and nonprofessional, skilled or unskilled. Who we are is not as important as who we desire to become regardless of where we are in life's great journey. Perhaps, more so than ever before, we are actually closer to becoming the architects of our own destiny...there are new EQUALIZERS!"

It is very logical to leverage underutilized assets into additional income sources, especially when we can. Flexibility in how we can work is now possible and a choice. You can choose the way you desire to work and make the decision yourself! Professional or non-professional, skilled or relatively skilled – when you know how to do something that is of value to others, you can now have more control of how you use your time and leverage what you have as an asset. A gig can be a starting point, a component of a new foundation for living and working.

I have personally interviewed hundreds of people who work in the gig economy, and I have found the stories to be amazing. My primary interest is to understand their motivation for working their gig and how long they have been working their gig. A few years ago, my Uber driver happened to be a former successful attorney from South Africa who decided he wanted to experience a change in the educational environment his sons were experiencing. He came to the United States knowing that he could find ways to work and earn in the gig economy. He had no fear of being unemployed as an attorney. The gig economy was his temporary equalizer.

Whenever we experience any form of economic uncertainty, it is natural for workers to become sensitive to the relationship between inflation and wages. Workers do not have any control over inflation. The facts are: **Most workers, in the traditional employer/employee relationship, have very little control over their wages once the initial agreements are made at the beginning of employment.** Performance Appraisals in the traditional workplace environment can recommend an accelerated increase in wages when excellence in performance is observed and measured. The insights provided in this book are not to critique a very successful and time-tested worker/employer relationship which has served all mature economies for many years. This book offers a new perspective. Our perspective honors the past while acknowledging and asserting that work and income earning possibilities can be viewed very differently.

Our perspective is based on the growing increase in individual entrepreneurship and flexible work opportunities and the following facts:

1. Less can be more.

2. Over 70 million Americans are engaged in flexible work they control. Most who are engaged in flexible work invest only a few hours per week.

3. We are not limited to one source of income as we once were in the earlier stages of the industrial economic work model.

Facts: The average and median increase in inflation in 2024 was **3.5%** over the prior year. The forecasted inflation rate for 2025 is now estimated to be between **2.2% to 2.5%.** The forecasted average increase in salaries for the typical worker is **3.5% to 3.9%.** When we use the higher of both forecasts, traditional salaried workers can expect a net gain of **1.4%.** The aforementioned figure reflects a rise in the value of work-related contribution. The question becomes: **Is this enough to motivate and inspire workers of any type?**

Insight: Whenever we realize that the **Return on Investment (ROI)** of monies saved or invested is less than what might be possible, we tend to adjust. Perhaps our most important measurement to watch is: **Our Return on Work Effort (ROWE).** The average worker will probably have a ROWE of 1.4% at the end of 2025 when dependent on one source of traditional income. When an incremental source of income is embraced that can yield $500.00 to $1,000.00 per month, working in a flexible manner, the ROWE immediately becomes 4% to 8% or much more when the incremental income exceeds $1,000.00 per month. The possibilities and choices have never been greater! Individual entrepreneurship is on the rise for very good reasons. **We can now develop multiple income sources without conflicting with or disturbing the core income source.**

We are always living in the best of times because we are living. To be able to enjoy the complexities and challenges of life is to enjoy the very gift we have been given. We must always make the most of what we have, or **we must invent what we would like to have.** Freedom of choice remains precious! Freedom of choice enables both possibilities and responsibilities.

Choices are EQUALIZERS. This equalizer is, perhaps, the most important; therefore, we will spend more time sharing our perspective on this EQUALIZER. Our research and thoughts have always been focused on why gigs fuel new values, such as the desire for more flexibility and freedom in how we work. There are solid reasons why a significant and diverse population gravitates toward work that focuses more on new attributes related to how the work is accomplished. We continue to move toward a 50% gig type participation in the workplace.

From this perspective, a growing percentage of job applicants will not be interested in traditional nine-to-five working hours. We have no way of estimating what will actually happen pertaining to the college graduating classes of 2025, however, personally, I would not be surprised if half of this new crop of college graduates will ever work a traditional job. Those whose skill set supports the growth of industries requiring specialized talent may find that their talent and skill set will remain valuable or of even greater value, however, these new graduates may work a bit differently than the traditional norm.

Many of us who are individual entrepreneurs are predicting a continued increase in the number of individual entrepreneurs. This will be fueled by the many new choices now available. The following is a direct lift from a simple google search:

"According to a 2024 Global Entrepreneurship Monitor (GEM) report, **levels of entrepreneurial activity are on the rise globally**. *New technologies, evolving customer demands, societal shifts, and the COVID-19 pandemic are rapidly changing the business landscape.* **582 million entrepreneurs exist worldwide in 2025**, *and small businesses and startups contribute significantly to the global economy. Young adults, particularly those ages 18 to 24, show the highest entrepreneurial activity and are leading the charge toward sustainability-focused businesses."*

The new choices truly shift the ownership of the work from the employer to the independent worker who now has as much control over when and how the work is to be done as the traditional employer. This amazing shift in ownership of the work changes many things including the definition of the worker. **New independent workers who work as free-lancers, gig workers, consultants, or advisors are now also considered Independent Entrepreneurs.**

Becoming an entrepreneur has traditionally meant a willingness to assume risk, often considerable risk in exchange for the opportunity to be in total control of a work opportunity and the possibility of fair rewards. The entrepreneurial story, foundational to the American story, and the attributes of free enterprise, have always enabled exciting possibilities. Ordinary people have accomplished extraordinary outcomes, building small and big businesses, some of which have become global brands. **The new Individual Entrepreneurs will accomplish more with less.**

In the most recent survey conducted by the *Ultimate Gig Project*, 69% of gig workers are now working multiple gigs. It is not unusual to find a real estate agent working an additional income possibility, a direct seller who may be working as a real estate agent or broker of something else, the teacher who mentors online and develop multiple clients, the professional who develops multiple clients by marketing a service strictly through a digital platform or works through a company like Upwork that connects those in need of services with a potential provider, a hobbyist who has turned a hobby into an ecommerce store via the support of a Shopify type platform or engagement with a platform like Etsy. The hospitality industry is loaded with freelance possibilities. Those participating in such activities are considered to be Independent Entrepreneurs, many of whom are considered Solopreneurs.

Today, as a result of vast innovation in technology, we can accomplish so much more with less. The concept of "less is more" is real. Because we can accomplish more in less time enables the possibility of engaging in multiple income opportunities. Choices are EQUALIZERS.

Flexibility is an EQUALIZER. Many of us have lived through times when, regardless of our experience or educational background, we could not leverage more hours into more possibilities because we could not find the flexibility we needed. Perhaps you have experienced a time when predefined work schedules did not fit within your life's constraints or conflicted with your chosen values, such as how you wished to care for your family. You may have experienced times when a flexible work arrangement would have served as a bridge between the last job and the next long-term opportunity you were pursuing. You may have determined you needed to work again after formally retiring because your retirement plan did not work as you had envisioned. Or you may have been looking for an entrepreneurial opportunity that offered minimal risk. Today's gig-providing companies have created what past generations hoped to find: flexible work opportunities that can be engaged by the masses. The dreams of yesteryear have become today's realities and possibilities.

The desire for flexibility is not new. Human Resource professionals have been working with the concept of flex time for approximately 15 or more years. It is not unusual to meet someone who now works a few days a week at the office and from home the balance of the week. Chances are, you have also met someone who works for an established company however, they never go to an office or fixed location. They work from home, and the hours are flexible. Many major corporations have taken the step of abandoning the office centric environment. The debate will continue as to how you maintain culture when people do not interact. We continue to value personal interaction; we simply do it differently. Video conference calls work and we have learned how to make them work more effectively.

Flexibility in how we work, when we work and from where we work enables freedom and choice. Parents can choose to work and take care of a family when the opportunity of flexibility can be engaged. Flexibility can enable better or more productive work and life balance allowing for more engagement in what we enjoy doing or the opportunity to leverage more of our precious time effectively. Flexibility can enhance family relationships when work can be interwoven into, or managed around, family responsibilities, goals, and objectives. Flexibility can enable both the opportunity to learn, study, and earn for students attempting to complete an education and work simultaneously. Flexibility can enable multiple streams of income creation when the objective is to earn more when reducing expenses is not an option. Flexibility may be the only way a person who is retired can close the gap between what was expected or envisioned vs what may have actually happened that was unexpected.

Most important to grasp from the perspectives being shared is being willing to embrace the opportunity to learn something new. Those who are products of the traditional work model of the industrial focused economy where work was defined in the traditional manner of spending a specific number of hours each day at a specific location five days a day with the promise of a vacation of a few weeks per year will benefit from reading this book. Our traditional routines easily become habits and habits are hard to escape from. Our habits can be barriers which prevent or handicap our beliefs in exploration and doing anything differently. The idea of retirement from anything does not have the same acceptable definition as it did for past generations. Why retire when one can re-fire and do something, possibly new and different, with the freedom and flexibility to learn at one's own pace and then explore and work as one desire. There are no limits to what we can learn to do when we are willing to renew our thinking, perhaps change our thinking, and embrace the idea of new possibilities. It is also wise to grasp from the perspectives being shared that we are no longer limited to the possibility of learning one thing. We can embraced multiple learning choices/possibilities/opportunities to determine which may fit best.

It is obvious that *flexibility* is a new value that all generations are applying to their work and income earning possibilities. For those who are experiencing being replaced or displaced in the traditional work environment, seeking a flexible work/income option could be the best preparation one might embrace. Downsizing is a label many organizations, companies, and even our government, have used to describe the opportunity to do more with less. This label is often perceived in a negative manner; however, it is a new reality. When traditional functions or processes can be accomplished with less investment of capital and labor, new opportunities and efficiencies are created. Technology has certainly been an enabler of new efficiencies and also new possibilities. Flexibility in how work can be done in a rewarding manner is an equalizer.

The Great Resignation of 2021 was real and remains real. Brian Chesky, founder and CEO of Air BnB, explained the value of flexibility to workers. Chesky stated: "Our company wants to attract the most talented into its ranks and the most talented may not always be living or even want to live in close proximity to the geography which our offices currently reside." Shopify CEO and co-founder Tobias Lutke announced in 2021 that he predicted the office centric era to be ending and therefore, Shopify employees would not return to an office centric environment. In March of 2022 (soon after the worst of the pandemic), Goldman Sachs CEO, David Solomon, insisted that all employees return to regular work hours five days a week. He provided a two-week notice, and several media outlets reported that about 50% showed up. What happened to those who did not show up? Many embraced new opportunities and possibilities.

Our reliance on physical interaction has now evolved. We do not discount the importance and value gained from physical interaction; however, we can no longer rely on the event/traditional job focused concept for exchange of information, discussion, and decision making. Speed is important therefore the speed at which we do all things pertaining to how we work and live has accelerated. Virtual calls and conferencing are no longer intriguing; they are an expectation. They can be scheduled to fit individual availability. Time zones and geography are no longer barriers. The flight and hotel expense is eliminated when the discussion needs to be timely. This applies to our personal lives as well as our work life. We do all of the essentials of living and working online to some degree, and the percentage of those who participate in online activities has grown rapidly. Example: Forbes reported a 55% increase in eCommerce overall since 2020. A trip to the shopping mall, once thought to be an exhilarating experience may not be described the same way today. It is simply not needed for many of our shopping needs when a digital mall or store is available 24/7.

Those who continue to debate the effectiveness of online relationships vs the need to meet personally may miss the most important evolution in communication in the last 2,000 years. From this perspective, there is no debate about the effectiveness of a personal/physical group gathering when feasible. However, the facts are: We now live in a digital economy where utilizing the tool of "online" is simply an absolute must! We shop online, we bank online, some of us even do Church online. Many of us now work online.

We will continue to emphasize attributes associated with the *NEW ECONOMY* as repetition typically stimulates thinking, which we know is so important when new decisions are being contemplated. As long as you are equipped with desire and determination, regardless of whether you are young or mature, you can find an equalizer which can be the beginning of a more entrepreneurial approach to life and work. The gig economy has also become a safety net for those who are displaced and replaced without warning.

Simplicity is an EQUALIZER! Simplicity is now a strategy. Less is more! Complexity is outdated or less preferred simply because simplicity is available. Consumers of goods and services seek simplicity in how they purchase or engage a service. Companies that provide goods and services can no longer ignore the value of a digital platform. A digital platform enables consumer client access to products and services 24/7 and there are no geographical barriers associated with where the store or office happens to be. The store is now everywhere. The trend and acceptance of eCommerce is one example of how dramatically many aspects of our living and working have changed.

Simplicity is all around us yet not so easy to adapt into one's personal life, be it work, business or other. Our common objective to effectively embrace and adhere to the basic wealth accumulation formula (earn more than we spend, save and invest the difference wisely) is easier said than accomplished. Habits prevail in many cases, and it becomes very difficult to change, innovate, or experiment with something new which may be uncomfortable. We tend to easily forget that every new course we have ever embraced in life was probably uncomfortable in the beginning. However, our pursuit of learning and experiencing something new enabled us to increase knowledge, develop, and perfect our skills, and/or gain a new experience.

Multiple income possibilities have never been greater. The idea of one single job or career engaged for a lifetime is a concept or value cherished by previous generations but not understood by younger generations.

Once a decision is made to enhance personal or family income, grow the organization or company, other decisions must be embraced relative to our new way of thinking, and how we will manage our time. Whenever we decide to do something that we probably have not done before, research, study, and a new way of thinking will probably become prerequisite. We always observe a strong tendency and reluctance to embrace a new idea or the process of innovation and transformation. This is true for individuals, companies, and organizations. **However, there is no "back to the future" strategy on record, to the best of our knowledge, which warrants exploration and investment in how we invent the future.**

Once the decision is made to do something different, to move forward, to embrace new growth possibilities, simplicity becomes of paramount importance. This rationale is based upon the importance of clarity and focus, avoidance of stress, anxiety, and disruption – all of which can lead to failure. Failure is not the worst thing in the world when disruption is avoided. We will simply try again!

Thoughtful embracement of a new idea should fit existing principles and values of importance. The embracement of the new idea should never be based solely upon a financial metric.

LEVERAGE is an EQUALIZER. Those embracing flexible work opportunities in any of its formats, and those who are becoming the new breed of *NEW ECONOMY* worker/

entrepreneur, are in pursuit of becoming the architects of their personal destiny. They are leveraging or seeking to leverage all or some of their assets. Assets can be tangible or intangible. As previously shared, assets can be physical assets such as homes, cars, tools, equipment, time, knowledge, education, and skills. Passion or purpose are also assets. These new independent entrepreneurs represent a diverse group inclusive of highly skilled professionals.

When leverage is embraced, it becomes an accelerator or possibly an equalizer! Leverage is also a process of understanding that we are not confined to "one thing" in our pursuit of work, career, happiness, and peace of mind. Human ingenuity continues to improve life. Leverage is a possibility for everyone regardless of age, past experience or inexperience.

Independent entrepreneurs are those who decide to bet on themselves. They are incorporating the concepts of leverage. This new breed of *NEW ECONOMY* entrepreneurs are the connectors between products and services and those who need those products and services. These intermediaries, also referred to as affiliates, independent contractors, freelancers, and microentrepreneurs, understand that their success depends upon the quality of products and services they provide to others. Their efforts are serving to enhance the value of brands. In a very technology focused world, these new independent entrepreneurs keep the importance of personal relationships and customer service at the forefront representing new and effective channels of distribution for companies providing products and services.

The concepts and insights expressed in this book represent new possibilities. Many of these possibilities did not exist 20 short years ago. Leverage is available to the masses as proven by over 70,000,000+ Americans who are already involved in the gig economy and/or some form of freelancing and involvement as an independent contractor.

New opportunities do not guarantee new possibilities.

Opportunities have to be leveraged into new possibilities.

Our review of the past reveals that the basic profile of society continues to remain about the same even when education becomes more available and new opportunities and possibilities far surpass those of a previous decade. **We realize that opportunities have to be chosen and embraced.** Awareness of the opportunity also plays a significant factor in being able to activate new possibilities. **When we are not aware that the opportunity exists it is impossible to activate a new possibility.**

Therefore we approach this book in a manner that we hope will enhance awareness. The primary prerequisite is mostly "desire" and determination to maximize the potential of the assets that we already have.

Leverage is a concept we associate with utilizing underutilized assets. Leverage can become a philosophy on which we can change the game of life/work balance. When inflation outpaces average wage increases by 2x or 4x, as we have experienced here in the United States, we can activate concepts of leverage to ensure against losses in purchasing power and actually accelerate attainment of goals and objectives.

The type of current work or profession we are currently engaged in should not interfere with an opportunity to leverage underutilized assets. The limitations of years past have been eliminated. The gig economy has changed the game and become an enabler of choice. We can choose what we would like to do and even try something new that we never explored before. Or we can develop an underutilized asset into the enterprise we often dreamed about but felt too risky to try. We can even develop a new career through multiple opportunities or possibly find the one thing we always knew was out there, we just didn't know exactly what it was or how to develop it. We can now work around other priorities without disrupting priorities. We can try something new without risking what we have established. We can enhance the work/life balance, perhaps, become the architect of our own destiny, or at least gain more control.

When new knowledge and thoughts enter into our thinking, we think differently. When we think differently, we can expect to impact outcomes differently.

Leveraging Your Assets is a Possibility

Individuals can now leverage assets beyond the traditional platform of the core job/career routine. The core form of employment is probably easier in many ways because technology has provided us with better and more efficient tools. Students learn faster and teachers teach more effectively as a result of technology. Our kids cannot imagine a phone that sat on a table or was fixed to a wall. What was that?

Therefore, it simply makes sense to leverage our assets to our advantage. We have the time to do so. We can choose to be solely focused on the traditional or we can explore the new possibilities without disrupting the core focus of personal and family responsibility.

Leverage Will Enable Multiple Income Streams

By engaging opportunities to develop multiple income streams, we easily assume that knowledge, skills, and experience will be enhanced, even passion and purpose. When we enhance and develop these areas we add value to who we are and what we are capable of doing. Our confidence in ourselves is likely to rise. Our control of total outcome and the return on our investments in work (ROWE) are likely to increase as we also gain confidence that one thing does not totally impact the total.

This could be an advantage gained from developing multiple income streams.

Because so many are now working multiple gigs, this may also be an indicator of a search for the right type of work in which we will invest even more time. Gigs allow you to try and if you do not like it, you simply move on. Switching gigs or taking on another gig does not trigger the emotional roller coaster of feelings activated when one moves from one job to another or experiences the loss of a primary job which necessitates the quest for a new income earning opportunity.

Building multiple income streams may be a first step in achieving entrepreneurial independence. Physical assets are no longer a prerequisite or essential. The assets to be leveraged are more digital and mental.

Because we discuss multiple income possibilities, and the trend to engage them, should not be interpreted to mean that this pathway is a recommended pathway. We have described the positive results that can be achieved. We did not describe the negative possibilities that could be experienced. Confusion or dilution of focus is also a possibility when objectives and clarity of purpose are not clearly defined and planned. It does not make sense to engage many different things because we can.

YOU are the most important EQUALIZER. We assert that we are living in the best of times amidst any current challenges we might tend to describe.... For those who seek to be more in control! The possibility to develop income streams that can be complementary to a primary source of income and/or build a new primary source as an Independent Entrepreneur are greater than we have ever experienced. However, choices do not mean anything if individuals do not choose. Therefore, EQUALIZERS are only important and impactful when individuals choose to become architects of their own destiny.

FINAL THOUGHTS – YOU ARE THE MAIN EQUALIZER
21st Century Leadership
By Stedman Graham

A key consideration in the 21st century is maintaining relevance in a constantly evolving and technologically advanced global marketplace.

The goal for 21st Century leadership is to keep changing the way we think and feel about our possibilities. As the world changes, we have to change with it. Innovation and creativity are ongoing and require strong leadership skills to maintain a competitive mindset.

Our opportunity is to understand who we are and become clear on our place in this world, to develop an identity which guides all the ways we think, feel, and move.

It took me a long time to understand that instead of trying to change the mindset of other people, our impact will be made when we change our own mindset.

Throughout the journey of self-discovery and trying to find out who I was, I learned that it is not how the world defines you that is important, but how you define yourself.

A fixed mindset is that we believe change is temporary; we cope with circumstances rather than forging possibilities by disrupting our fears. If you don't learn to work through unfamiliar situations, you will find it difficult to progress in a rapidly evolving world.

Identity and leadership is necessary in the mist of global challenges; the anxiety associated with uncertainty due to the change process proves a focus on emotional intelligence is required in leadership today to create a sustainable work / life balance.

Change or a growth mindset requires a vision, planning and the seizing of opportunity.

Change also involves an emotional tie as getting beyond your comfort zone is always daunting. This is an emotional process because nobody likes to surrender the comfort associated with our beliefs, values, and identities. We become skeptical and reluctant to embrace change and overcome our fears.

Today, the evidence is everywhere. In no other time in history has there been a greater need for people to be leaders of their own lives and claim their rights as human beings, which includes the freedom to achieve their full potential. Good leadership, or lack thereof, determines the success or failure of an individual or organization.

Never have the peoples of our world had a greater need for identity and leadership.

Great leadership is about competence and influence, the ability to grow other people's support – regardless of whether you are seeking to build a clientele or contributing to an organization. People follow leaders they believe in and who demonstrate values with which they align. Leaders know they cannot change others only themselves.

The best way to predict your future is to create it.

We live in a global world connected by technology where most things are possible. We have new possibilities and opportunities. What is missing is how to apply the opportunity to us. There is a saying "Success is when preparation meets opportunity." The preparation is learning how to empower ourselves so we can sort the information, knowledge, and education and make it relevant to our development.

Working in community and corporate America, leading nonprofits, and speaking throughout the world for more than 30 years, developing a formidable reputation for helping corporations, organizations and individuals succeed. In all that time, I have come to know one thing: Leadership is everything. Identity leadership is the highest order of leadership. It is likely to become the "different kind of leadership" that is required in the 21st Century. – found in people as high potentials who are aware of their own intentions and identity, who responsibly lead themselves to overcome obstacles in their lives, and, as a result, lead others to succeed in driving organization's growth. You are not your circumstances; you are your possibilities.

Stedman Graham is the author of *Identity Leadership*. The book is driven by his proprietary Nine Step Success Process which is based on the philosophy that you cannot lead anyone else until you first lead yourself.

PERSPECTIVE
Healthcare in the *NEW ECONOMY*
Meeting People Where They Are
By Phil Chrysler, President & CEO of Impact Health Sharing

The following contribution provides a very unique perspective focused on one of the most important components of our living and working: Access to the health care we need at affordable pricing. We have intentionally placed this perspective behind the Chapter – *NEW ECONOMY*/NEW EQUALIZERS.

I have been working with the direct selling channel of distribution for many years. My wife and I, having been successful with the direct selling model, can easily remember the "fear" of working our business full-time because we were afraid of losing the group insurance benefits provided by our employers. Ironically, we have always been conscious of the importance of maintaining healthy habits – healthy diet and consistent exercise, ... the things that we could control. As I now reflect on our personal fears at that time,

I also saw those fears in many others who were simply afraid of becoming an independent entrepreneur. Eventually we took the leap, and we found a way to obtain the insurance coverages we needed. We also paid premium prices because we were no longer eligible for group rates.

As we have mentioned many times, the *NEW ECONOMY* will drive innovation, transformation and change in the manner in which we do many things in our living and working. We recently became aware of the concept of "health sharing." This new and very different approach to health care embraces a very different and innovative option, especially for *NEW ECONOMY* Entrepreneurs. We are delighted to bring you the following perspective.

Healthcare in America is at a crossroads. For decades, the prevailing model has been employer-sponsored insurance, where individuals are grouped together, and premiums are set based on collective risk. While this system has worked for many, it often fails to account for individual health choices and circumstances. If you're healthy and lead an active lifestyle, you're still contributing monthly to the collective pool. This one-size-fits-all approach doesn't reward personal health investments.

At the same time, the workforce is changing. Millions of Americans are stepping away from traditional employment, embracing independent work, self-employment, and entrepreneurial ventures. Independence brings freedom, flexibility, and creative opportunity, but it also brings new challenges, especially when it comes to healthcare. Individual health insurance options are often expensive, restrictive, and misaligned with people's lives. High-cost premiums and deductibles, narrow networks, and confusing bureaucratic systems and red tape leave many feeling anxious, overburdened, and frustrated—even when they are paying more than ever for their health insurance.

The financial consequences are real. A 2024 analysis by the Kaiser Family Foundation found that in the U.S. approximately 14 million adults (6% of the population) owe over $1,000 in medical debt, with about 3 million adults (1%) owing more than $10,000[1]. Adding another dimension to this crisis, over 57% of U.S. hospitals' bad debt in 2022 came from insured patients[2]. This shift underscores that medical debt is not solely an issue for the uninsured—insured Americans are increasingly carrying significant financial burdens, highlighting systemic gaps in affordability and access.

As the workforce evolves, with more individuals embracing independent work and entrepreneurship, the traditional healthcare model becomes increasingly misaligned with their needs. These independent workers seek healthcare solutions that align with their lifestyles, reward healthy living, and offer flexibility and more control over their healthcare experience. It's time for healthcare that puts people first, not profits, the way it should be.

The Human Impact

At its core, healthcare is about human experience, not just policy and premiums. The current systems can often create stress, anxiety, and confusion for the very people it is meant to serve. Independent workers, freelancers, and small business owners juggle unpredictable incomes, long hours, and personal responsibility while trying to maintain their health.

This human dimension cannot be overlooked. Healthcare is more than a financial product; it is a foundation for living, working, and thriving. Bureaucracy, administrative hurdles, and opaque pricing make it harder for people to access timely care or to proactively manage their wellness. When healthcare feels complicated and punitive, it undermines both individual and societal well-being.

---

1 https://www.kff.org/health-costs/the-burden-of-medical-debt-in-the-united-states

2 https://www.theguardian.com/us-news/2024/jan/11/hospital-debt-increase-people-with-insurance

The Need for Innovation

The *NEW ECONOMY* demands new solutions. Healthcare must evolve to reflect the realities of independent work, modern lifestyles, and proactive wellness. People need options that are flexible, affordable, and tailored to their circumstances. This is not about replacing traditional insurance entirely—it is about creating alternative modern solutions that empower people to take control of their health while supporting their financial stability.

Healthcare innovation can take many forms:

- **Proactive Wellness:** Annual wellness visits and routine labs are designed to help people stay ahead of their health. Early detection and preventive care lead to better long-term outcomes—encouraging individuals to take an active role in their well-being.

- **Lifestyle-Aligned Incentives:** Healthcare should recognize the intentional choices people make every day. By rewarding preventive care, regular exercise, and healthy living, it shifts from simply managing risk to supporting healthier, more empowered lives.

- **Accessible, Purposeful Technology:** Modern healthcare leverages telehealth, digital tools, and AI-driven solutions to make care more convenient, and efficient. Technology helps individuals easily navigate care on their terms, wherever they live and work.

- **Simplified Administration:** Bureaucracy and red tape can be as challenging as the health issues themselves. Simplifying processes, paperwork, and approvals allows people to focus on health rather than administrative hurdles.

- **Transparent Cost and Quality:** Clear, upfront information empowers individuals to make informed decisions. Eliminating surprise costs and confusing restrictions ensures people know exactly what they are getting and their financial responsibility.

- **Trusted Patient-Provider Relationships:** Care works best when providers are empowered to make decisions based on their expertise—not constrained by corporate mandates or utilization reviews. Trusting providers to know what's right for their patients ensures better outcomes and improves the overall healthcare experience for both patients and clinicians.

These innovations are not futuristic—they are increasingly demanded by a workforce that values independence, flexibility, and empowerment.

Rewarding Health, Not Risk

For too long, the healthcare system has operated as a one-size-fits-all risk pool. Healthy people subsidize higher-cost care for others without receiving any recognition or reward. In the *NEW ECONOMY*, this approach is increasingly misaligned with people's expectations and values. Shouldn't healthcare reflect the choices people make to live well? Shouldn't proactive health behaviors be incentivized?

Independent workers are showing how autonomy and responsibility can reshape industries. Healthcare must follow suit. By creating solutions that reward healthy lifestyles, we can align financial incentives with human behavior, resulting in better outcomes for both individuals and society.

Meeting People Where They Are

The future of healthcare in the *NEW ECONOMY* is about meeting people where they are—financially, geographically, and behaviorally. Independent workers are diverse, with variable incomes, schedules, and health profiles. They need solutions that are personalized, flexible, and empowering and that put them at the forefront, not profits.

This is a human-centered approach: understanding the day-to-day realities of people's work, recognizing the challenges of managing health independently, and creating systems that support thriving rather than merely insuring against catastrophe.

A Vision for the Future

The *NEW ECONOMY* is here. Millions are embracing independent work, creating opportunity, and redefining success on their own terms. Healthcare should not remain tethered to outdated, industrial-era employment models. It must evolve to reflect today's human needs, lifestyles, and choices.

The opportunity is clear: healthcare can reward healthy living, simplify access, and empower individuals to thrive, without being constrained by bureaucracy or profit motives. Leaders and innovators in healthcare have a responsibility to design solutions that prioritize health, reduce stress, and empower people to succeed.

For independent workers, this means care that is affordable, transparent, and aligned with how they live. For society, it means fewer financial emergencies and less medical debt. For the economy, it means a workforce that is healthier, more resilient, and more productive.

The challenge is significant, but the vision is compelling. As we step into this future, let us create healthcare that meets people where they are, values the choices they make, and rewards them for living well. That is the promise of the *NEW ECONOMY*—and it is a promise worth pursuing.

CHAPTER 5
RELEVANCE IS REQUISITE

When explaining innovative ideas I often reference principles learned during my study of architecture. Buildings and structures are not accidentally built. They are the result of methodical planning and an adherence to solid and proven engineering and construction principles. Once a building is designed and the planning for construction is complete, the building can be built, and the structure may last a few hundred years or more.

The processes associated with the way we live and the way we work are not as rigid as the process used to design, plan, and construct a building. Therefore, it is critically important that we embrace an understanding that "changes" will always be an essential part of our living and working. Much has changed over the past few years and more will change over the next few. What becomes most important is our commitment to remain relevant. In order to remain relevant, we change, adapt, and often need to innovate and renovate. Sometimes, we are forced to address the possibility of needing to reinvent. Just as buildings that have experienced years of service to the people and communities which use them are often renovated, the same appears to be required of the manner in which we live and work.

Wherever you are at this moment in time, you are in precisely the right moment. This simple belief structure that I've held throughout my life has enabled me to understand situations better and seek learning from any of my disappointments. I have experienced what it feels like when forced to change to avoid the loss of relevance. I have also experienced what it feels like to lead innovation and change both personally and professionally. The relevant never watch what is happening, they embrace the need to change and seek to become more relevant.

I also understand the pain associated with change. When humans are involved, many will always resist change for assorted reasons; some of the reasons are valid and full of learning. Some of the reasons as to why others resist change will never be understood. An undesirable situation warrants change. The undesirable situation can be related to how we are living and working and whether we are growing in pursuit of our objectives. Organizations and corporations experience the exact same thing only in a different manner. Stability is seldom a long-term rationale for a situation that is not growing. We often recognize the need for change and then we take the position that we do not want to change, an untenable paradox that can easily lead to becoming less valuable to ourselves, our families and the companies and organizations in which we are involved.

Jim Rohn, speaker, author, and business coach whose work and articulation of entrepreneurial and motivational principles, values, and concepts are forever etched on my mind and the minds of millions of others, said, "For things to change, you have to change." This is absolutely true. Yet, in today's collaborative world where it takes teams pulling in the same direction to succeed, perhaps a one-word edit is prudent. "For things to change, 'we' need to change." Rohn's intent remains, but its strength is multiplied exponentially, especially for those who seek to remain relevant.

I am motivated to share my thoughts on the subject because it is my deep belief that we, as humans, are ingenious. It is amazing what we can overcome and accomplish when we believe that we can. Therefore, it is important to recognize the moment we are in as an opportunity, or even "a calling," to rise to challenges never before encountered, meet them, and becomes the architects of something actually better than what we currently experience. I shared the quote below at the beginning of this book and now I share it again...

> "And whether or not it is clear to you, no doubt the universe is unfolding as it should. Therefore be at peace with God, whatever you conceive Him to be. And whatever your labor and aspirations, in the noisy confusion of life, keep peace in your soul. With all its sham, drudgery, and broken dreams, it is still a beautiful world. Be cheerful. Strive to be happy."

— Max Ehrmann © 1927

Be Aware of the Following

1. **Ignoring data analytics** – Data often provide the first warning signals. When we ignore data, we miss the opportunity to develop learning and insights. We can attempt to "course correct" via artificial means or minimize the value of data. For instance, organizations and businesses often use incentives to offset less than desirable metrics. When they do, the question to ask is: Do incentives increase the value of what is being done, spur sustainable performance, or simply provide a carrot that when replicated too often takes on the effect of an addictive drug? Individuals can easily ignore the metrics associated with the amount earned vs the amount saved and invested.

2. **Excuses/Denial** – One of my favorite books is *Good to Great* written many years ago by Jim Collins. The content of the book transcends the time in which it was written. Chapter 4 in that book, which outlines the pursuit of greatness that distinguishes great companies from other companies, emphasizes the necessity of confronting the brutal facts! The same is true for individuals.

3. **Chasing Ducks** – This is an expression that I've heard others use on many occasions and one that I prefer over "spinning wheels." Both expressions are simplistic ways to describe a situation analysis indicating that what is going on is simply not working.

   As a kid, I remember venturing to a large park that contained a big pond where ducks swam during certain seasons of the year. Whenever I saw the ducks, I wanted to catch one. Why? I do not know. Whenever I got close to a duck, it would simply fly away. I was a kid doing what kids do, but individuals and organizations of all kinds chase their fair share of ducks. Sticking to plans that once worked but do not continue to work, is a form of chasing ducks.

   Individuals, organizations, and companies that depend on people to embrace a product or service are wise to focus on relevance. When we stop serving people in a relevant manner, we become irrelevant.

   Individuals, organizations, and companies that prefer attempts to reinvent the past are probably chasing ducks.

4. **No identifiable progress toward goals/planned objectives** - Progress toward a goal or objective is easy to measure. One only has to monitor the Key Performance Indicators. This is not rocket science. This simple analysis is equally important to the Church or school, non-profit or for-profit organization, independent contractor, business consultant, entrepreneur, small business, or big business. This is not a theory or concept that is difficult to understand. The stats and facts tell a story. Everyone serious about building something significant has put into place analytics and metrics that are intended to be reviewed on a regular basis. However, it is possible for organizations and companies, independent contractors/independent entrepreneurs, workers of any type to ignore their key performance indicators. It is easy to continue to do the same thing even when we know the same things we have always done even though they are no longer working.

5. **Continuing to celebrate past performance** – I enjoy sharing thoughts on this one because throughout my life/work journey, I have experienced many accomplishments, and through it all I have never celebrated too long. I was taught to always understand and believe that the future is more important than the past. This previous statement does not infer that recognition for outstanding achievement is not important because it certainly is. Sure, I enjoy looking at some of the trophies and plaques awarded in the past as our nature is to appreciate recognition for outstanding performance. I kept a few plaques and trophies to decorate the shelves; however, the lessons learned from my failures, of which there were many, bear equal weight. We do not receive trophies for failures, but the experiences are etched in our minds.

   What's important here is that the past is not to be repeated, not our brilliance nor our blunders. Both pave the way for ongoing progress. Therefore, celebrating too long and placing too much value on past successes ignores the precarious nature of relevance in the present. Such a mindset certainly makes it difficult to create a relevant future.

6. **Continuing to support complexity vs simplicity.** It has always puzzled me why anyone, or any organization or business model embraces complexity? It may be hard to believe and illogical, but many do. Consumers, constituents, customers in all formats, intermediaries in all formats, every form of entrepreneur, all desire to be relevant; however, examples of how complexity is embraced can be found everywhere. But it's simplicity's successes that we remember and there are solid reasons why.

   The future of work has progressed, thanks to trending simplification. The gig economy illustrates "proof of concept" that work can be performed in a way that enables workers to have more flexibility and freedom vs the traditional work formats of the past 100 years. The growth and continued forecasted growth of the gig economy over the next few years emphasizes the appeal of simplicity, ease of engagement, and rewards based strictly on performance.

7. **Ignoring the impact of the digital economy.** The digital economy now impacts just about everything we do. We can shop online 24/7, meet with people w/o being there via virtual technology with no geographic or time-zone constraints. In other words, the world has changed, forcing us to change, adapt, transform, or possibly reinvent who we are. What was relevant only a few years ago may not be relevant today.

Positive Actions to Ensure Relevance

1. **Study the Situation** – Do not ignore the facts or the data. It is important to study, form insights, conduct additional research if needed, study more and form more insights. It is simply amazing how individuals, organizations, and companies can ignore the opportunities that "study" can offer to any situation analysis.

2. **Honest Self-Assessment** – Self-assessment is hard. No one wants to admit that they may be ineffective. There is always the excuse and/or the hope that normalcy will return. Sometimes it will but most often, it may not. There is nothing relevant or realistic about the thought…"*Back to the Future.*" The preceding was a good movie at one time; however, it is not deemed to be the essence of good thinking. Be honest with yourself.

3. **Act -** The solution lies in being big enough and smart enough to assess honestly. In organizations and companies, culture is everything. Failing to address the situation can lead to lost trust and talent…unnecessarily.

   a. Embrace the moment - Embracing the moment vs defending the condition activates energy and creativity. Excellent leaders appear to thrive on moments which require analysis, study, insightful thinking, collaboration, transformation... and possibly change. By sharing the moment, new possibilities are activated.

b. Create New Plans Based Upon Analysis and Solid Strategic Thinking. Moving an organizational or business model in a different direction requires thoughtful planning and often new learning. New plans cannot be approached without a keen understanding of what is and is not working; otherwise, new plans can easily be repetitive of old plans, just adjusted to make them look like new plans.

c. Realistic transformative strategy requires diligence, research, and study. This new learning takes time, as it requires "stepping outside" of the existing sandbox. Moving the sand around within the same box may provide a different appearance, but the substance remains the same. Strategic and realistic transformation plans should accomplish more than simply "moving stuff around."

Be Strategic About Your Next Steps

Failure to invest in analysis and a strategic planning process may be the costliest expense never recorded. What will be missed is considered essential to growth and avoidance of any form of irrelevance. The importance of *Clarity, Focus and Execution* were first made very clear to me by business strategist Tony Jeary who is known for his success in being a very effective business coach. Tony's clients include some very well-known CEOs of major corporations. Tony has a studio in Flower Mound, Texas. When you enter the main conference room you see, in huge letters across one of the conference room walls, the words *Clarity, Focus, Execution*. In the paper we wrote together, *Growth the Most Important Key Performance Indicator,* Tony elaborates on the importance of *Clarity, Focus and Execution*. I echo the importance with the following definitions lifted from the paper we wrote together.

CLARITY: Having clarity means being clear on vision, mission, objectives, and the resources needed to achieve desired results. If all business leaders clearly understood these terms and how powerfully they impact their organizations, there would likely be fewer failures. However, the reality is that most businesses experience both success and failure in achieving specific objectives during specific measurement periods. We also know that 50% of all startup businesses will no longer exist after five years. That percentage increases to more than 65% after ten years. Of course, we have no way of knowing what percentage of those companies failed to seek strategic clarity and focus which may have led to a different outcome.

FOCUS: Clear focus on what matters most eliminates wasted and unproductive effort, wasted capital, and loss of the organization's primary asset—it's best people. We have identified the following areas of focus that we consider essential and critical: People are always the first area of focus—the most important asset that never shows up on the balance sheet. It is the performance of the people within the organization, of course, that ultimately determines the performance of the organization. Having the right people on the team helps determine an organization's vibe, which is the essence of its culture. High performing organizations are a result of a high-performance culture.

EXECUTION: Effective execution is dependent upon clarity and focus on what matters most. Effective execution is never accidental, nor is it the result of simply developing a forecast and then doing what has always been done. The quarterly reports of many privately owned organizations and the filings of many publicly traded businesses are loaded with justifications for flawed execution that did not achieve forecasted targets and objectives. Our focus on execution starts with the formation of the strategic action plan, which includes optimization of processes. Great execution includes the component of speed. Increasing speed is possible when an organization embraces and optimizes duplicatable processes. Execution should be about implementation of the strategic plan. The absence of clear strategic objectives will often lead to the use of incentives, which can only influence results temporarily. Flawless execution can be possible when an organization's leaders clearly understand how to invest their time, people, and resources into the activities that yield the greatest returns in a sustainable manner, which supports sustainable growth.

Manage The Inflection Point

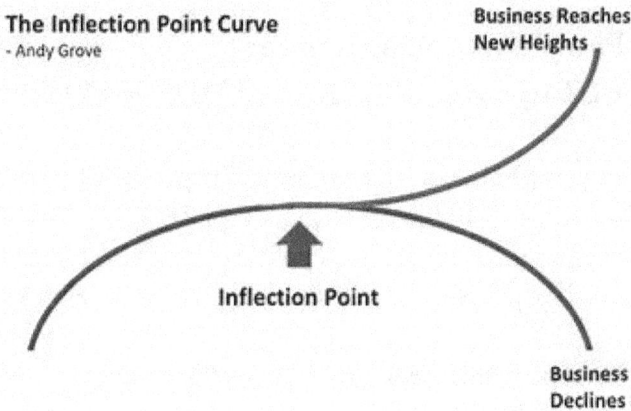

The Inflection Point Curve
- Andy Grove

Business Reaches New Heights

Inflection Point

Business Declines

We often hear the phrase "Inflection Point" used to describe a critical situation, whereby decisions and actions can make a significant difference between new opportunities to grow or experience the opposite of growth. Individuals, organizations, and companies all face inflection points where past successes have very little impact on the degree of success the future holds. Legacies are comprised of a laundry list of successes which are always important to the overall history of an entity or person. However, we have learned that prolonged celebrations of past performance often negate the actions necessary to attain the necessary current performance goals for sustained growth goals and objectives. So, legacy is equal parts success story and those actions that bring innovative ideas and research to the forefront, shaping past performance with research and ideas that form new actions and new growth strategies.

As I think about the next few years, pathways to choice and opportunity will no doubt open wider for relevant individuals and organizations, more so than any other period in my personal past. Individuals will continue to have more choices which support their ability to become architects of their own destinies. For the individual, it is not so much a matter of what is possible, but rather why and how they choose to participate in those possibilities. Business—small and large—will benefit from relevant individuals, who place value on research and study, strategic thinking and planning, ideas, and long-term solutions vs the temporary "fix" that satisfies "status quo."

Serve People in a Manner that Attracts, Engages, Retains...ADDS VALUE!

Serve the people means that we serve the people who engage our brand. Not some of the people who we place into self-described/defined categories, ... all of the people. Serving also means that we strive to serve the people beyond the actual product or service we offer.

As an Independent Entrepreneur/Owner of your work, whatever it may be, the quality of the service you render will have a direct impact on the quality of the relationship. This is true when interacting with your clients, customers, and brand partners.

Add Value means that we focus on providing all of the people engaged with our brand with the opportunity to gain directly from what we offer and indirectly from our principles and values and our understanding of who is in our audience.

When we serve the people and add value, we increase the likelihood that we will **grow the business or organization**, whatever it might be. When we infer that we serve the people and add value ... we imply the need for understanding the people who are in our audience and the need for clarity in thinking and the prerequisite of a well thought out plan for accomplishing growth objectives. One cannot expect to serve people and add value arbitrarily…it must be done strategically and intentionally.

As I recently thought about what matters most, as I reflected on many years of direct and indirect involvement with a variety of business models, it became obvious to me that nothing can be more important than understanding the people who are involved. Consequently, we developed a list of potential topics that are the focus of this perspective.

This perspective is about the people who may be involved as consumers, intermediaries or decision makers within the entities that may be referred to as a business or organization. Without people, it is difficult to describe the entity regardless of type or label. Therefore, it is rather logical when we state that the business or organization grows or ceases to grow based upon how effective we are in engaging and serving people. When we serve the people by meeting their needs, it is rather easy to develop the following hypothetical: **Those who serve the needs of people will benefit from the choices people will make when selecting the products, services, and opportunities they need.** If the preceding were easy to execute, there would be no failures, only successes and growth.

Through your reading of the following pages, perhaps you will be able to view your personal situation through a different lens. Why do we find it to be so very difficult to start, mange, or lead a business or organization that basically exists to serve the needs of people? If we manufacture the finest pet food, we still have to convince the people who own the pets that we offer pet food their pets will love. Pets do not make purchases even though they may make choices. My point: Growth is always about how effective we are in satisfying the needs of the people. When we serve the people, we can also expect to add value to the relationship and consequently, we grow as an individual, business, or organization.

However, there is also a "real world" whereas profits can be elusive, performance can falter, planned key performance indicators are missed, and the organization or business experiences something less than growth. Stagnation or lack of growth are not only possibilities, either can become reality. When the latter happens, we look for the answers and often miss the analysis. We can easily assume that we know what the audience needs because the response of the audience is less than what we anticipated, not necessarily whether we served the needs of the audience or not. We often manufacture complexity when simplicity may offer solutions.

Thoughts: We are not talking about customer satisfaction or measuring customer satisfaction accurately. If an individual, business, or organization is not attracting new members or customers, it may be necessary to identify factors affecting how potential customers view the offerings. The value proposition may no longer be understood or appealing and it may be perceived to be less meaningful than in prior years. The marketplace changes and often, it changes rapidly.

All of the preceding thoughts may trigger your thinking, eventually your planning and focus on what really matters most in ensuring that your choices and plans are best positioned to support growth. It is wise to remember that basically anything can be sold to a customer one time. However, the fact that the customer or member bought it one time should not lead to an assumption that they are satisfied enough to risk you again. In order for your audience to continue to "buy-in" you must serve the people in your audience but first and foremost, you must understand who they are.

Recognize the Personal Needs of Others

People are not one dimensional. People will determine their priorities by how they perceive "what matters most" at the particular moment in time when they are asked to examine priorities or offered opportunities. When we commit to serving people, we have to commit to understanding "what matters most" to the audience we are attempting to embrace and grow. This is a very challenging task because people are very diverse in how they think about what matters most.

We can easily fall into the trap of perceiving that "what matters most" is actually the organization, product, or service that we represent. However, this cannot be true other than for the moment(s) immediately following the introduction of the product or service simply because there are too many components of living and working that impact on the lives of people every day. In order to elevate any "one thing" to lasting priority status requires that we understand the people. When we do not truly understand people, we can easily fall into the trap of being solely focused on "**selling**" something vs "**solving**" a problem or fulfilling ongoing priorities and needs.

When we solve a problem or fulfill a need for someone else, through a personal effort, organizational effort, product, or service that we offer, we hope to gain an informed member, customer/client who will automatically perceive us as being relevant.

Generally, the provider of a product or service knows their product or service very well. However, the question that we present to providers is: How well do you understand the people in your audience who you target as potential members, buyers, and affiliates of your brand? The audience is generally very diverse. Data analysis will reveal how many of the new buyers actually change their minds within the first 24 hours or first 5 days. Further analysis will reveal how many new buyers received communication from the company within the first hours of engagement, first days, first week(s). Analysis will also reveal what new buyers think about the products/services they purchased. Analysis can also reveal how many new buyers place another order within their first 30 to 90 days of involvement and quite possibly why (real or hypothetical) the buyer is no longer engaged. What percentage do we actually retain? What was the cost of acquisition? Are we investing in retention, growing the customer base through satisfaction and ultimately referrals or are we assuming that we have a customer when we only acquired a transactional buyer?

People Have 5 Basic Needs

1. **People Have Mental Needs;** however, many are actually consumed by negativity.

2. **People Have Physical Needs** and some of the people are simply tired and physically drained. Health and Wellness is a hot topic. It is virtually impossible to maintain a positive mental attitude about anything when the body is simply tired.

3. **People Have Spiritual Needs/A Need For Belonging.** People want to have faith in themselves and the possibilities they encounter that support their desire to make life and work a bit better.

4. **People Have Social Needs.** People desire a connection with a community that they perceive cares about them.

5. **People Have Financial Needs.** The facts are: Many people are spending more than they earn.

The 5 elements of life that we identified as being important may not be a complete list. However, it is a good starting list when seeking to better understand how to motivate and inspire people to engage and stay with your brand. The 5 elements may have nothing to do with the product or service that you may offer but your understanding of what matters most to a vast majority of the typical audience has everything to do with whether or not you attract and retain people to become a part of your audience. Initial attraction can be the result of a transaction but ongoing growth in affiliation with your brand and lifetime value will be more related to how you serve the people involved.

Key Thought: When you understand the needs of the people and incorporate those needs in your value proposition, through your principles, values, and behaviors, you add value.

Add Value

There are many different business and organizational models. Some are based upon a "knock your socks off product or service that is quite unique," and these are actually very rare. Some businesses offer distinctions that you would not typically find someplace else such as personalization/customization to some degree or even a rare quality of product or service. When it comes to automobiles, the Ford/Chevy models are considered very different from the Rolls Royce or Bentley models. However, all of the models will transport passengers from one point to another. The question becomes; what is the magic sauce that leads to success regardless of whether the product is a Rolls or a Chevy? Is it to bring forth the most amazing product or service or is it more so about bringing forth the most amazing way to personalize the manner in which you serve the people? The choice between a Rolls or Chevy is obviously financial in nature, however, both prospective audiences have to be attracted and engaged.

We can add value to the relationships with members and customers when we understand our purpose and our audience. The automobile example used in the previous paragraph clearly implies that we must understand the audience. The Chevy/Ford audience probably cannot afford the Rolls or Bentley, so we do not waste time trying to sell a Rolls Royce to a Chevy audience. However, organizations and companies are chasing ducks all the time. Chasing Ducks is our way of expressing that type of activity that cannot lead to a positive outcome. We can chase ducks all day in an attempt to capture a duck. However, the chances are very slim that we will catch a duck through ordinary or traditional activity. When we chase a duck, the duck will simply fly away.

Experience appears to reveal that we add value to a relationship when we are able to satisfy and exceed the expectations and needs of the other person or audience. The relationship grows in value as expectations and needs are consistently achieved and exceeded. When expectations and needs are no longer achieved, the relationship(s) often terminates. This is true for a marriage, a friendship, a relationship with an organization or business. So, the question becomes; How do we add value to the relationship?

We share 5 thoughts that can be integrated into growth strategies that serve the purpose of adding value to the relationship so essential to growing the business or organization. As you read our thought-starters, you will also add your own.

These Thoughts/Actions Add Value

1. **Be grateful and demonstrate your gratitude** in the communication you have with the customer or member. The cost is zero. You are investing and betting on the power of language and the impact that words have on the other person. You are always grateful that others have chosen you to provide a product or service.

2. **Remind the audience consistently of your purpose to serve them in a manner that always meets and exceeds their expectations.** When you act in this manner, you also create accountability for delivering on the promises you make. It's a win-win strategy.

3. **Consistently share specific objectives for what you intend to accomplish through the relationship and the principles and values you adhere to.** If you are providing a product or service that saves time and money, repeat the assertion frequently and hold yourself accountable. If you are enhancing some specific aspect of the other person's life, state the assertion clearly and remind them often. People tend to forget.

Reminder: People want to have fun! If you can add some fun to the lives of those in your audience, you add value. This is often attempted through incentives and recently through gamification techniques. However, this can also be accomplished through simple recognition and storytelling of someone who has acknowledged satisfaction and enjoyment related to the experience you provided. The thoughts that we have provided are simply thought starters. They do not require investment of marketing dollars; they only require that you demonstrate what you value. By doing so, you add value to the lives of those in your audience and those you plan to bring into your audience.

Principles and Values often hang on the walls of executive offices or are found in the annual reports that publicly traded companies publish each year. Where are the principles and values during the other 364 days each year? Are they merely hanging on the walls of offices or are they within the mindset of every member of the organization or company – business of any size? What is the stated purpose and commitment of the individual, organization, or business? When the preceding are actually clearly communicated and within your mindset and that of every member of the organization or enterprise, large or small, the entity has a rudder that serves to help with the navigation required to weather the storms and the smooth seas which support the faster ride, always in the planned direction.

In the next paragraph we will create a hypothetical organization that maintains a focus on its purpose and its principles and values. Our hypothetical summary of an organization/business purpose might be:

> *The quality of the products and services you receive from us are most important. We do not want to disappoint you! Our commitment is to your total satisfaction. We also know that your life is composed of many other products and services that you also need. From time to time we will send you messages and newsletters. Our messages and newsletters will always remind you of what we have to offer, however, we will also remind you of other aspects of your life and work that we know to be important.*

> *We may be your chosen **shoelace** provider; however, we are so much more!*

Our purpose, principles and values can extend what we offer beyond the actual product or service that we provide. This thought applies to the company and the organization.

It is most important for the Individual Entrepreneurs seeking to build a business distinguishing them as being more personal!

Return on Value Added Behaviors

By focusing on the quality of your serving effort, you activate possibilities which can impact your objectives to grow the people that you are targeting as buyers, customers, or members. When you understand the people, you have a better chance of serving the people beyond expectations. When you accomplish this objective, you activate the possibility that a satisfied customer or member will share their satisfaction with others. By serving people beyond expectations, they may decide that you are worth their investments of time and money, possibly a source of increased income if they are seeking affiliation with a brand, or they may have been looking to simply affiliate with a product, service, or membership that they believe will enhance the quality of their life. When you touch people in this manner, they will share with others what was shared with them. The previous statement may be hypothetical; however, it is worthy of your thoughts and perhaps your belief.

The quality of your serving effort includes the value of your product or service as perceived by the audience, but the value of your serving effort also includes the manner in which you communicate and the value of the content, as perceived by your audience, within your marketing, communication, and the quality of the service you provide. Value creation requires that you go beyond what you actually offer in your product or service.

Example: I personally sought a quality protein supplement powder, plant based and diary free that was also loaded with good nutrition. I have challenges digesting various forms of protein, so I was also looking for a product that my digestive system would easily digest without undesirable side effects. I asked a few friends for recommendations, and I was led to an excellent product that met and exceeded my expectations. It has now been three years of consistently using this product and ordering every month. I subscribed to the monthly subscription opportunity to enjoy a discount. I have remained a customer, not only due to the quality of the product that I found, but also because of the quality of service the company provides. When I call Customer Service, someone answers the phone, and my questions are answered. I am sure that the Customer Service Reps work from home, however, the company evidently ensures that their customer service reps are competent - well acquainted with the product and trained with a focus on serving. I am also rewarded for my continuous purchasing which has led to me trying other products that I can try for free. When I receive updates and newsletters, I am reminded of many things that I can do to manage my objective to live as healthy as possible. I also receive a fresh "thank you note" for each order that I place. It has been and continues to be a remarkable experience in being the beneficiary of not only an excellent product but excellent service that adds value to the relationship.

I was also recently asked if I had realized how Amazon Prime Membership had increased in price from several years ago. My response was quite simple: I don't really care what the price is because it is certainly well worth it in terms of the time that I save. Amazon delivers on its promise to serve you well! The preceding is simply my expression of my personal experience. Amazon service excellence has propelled it to be one of the largest corporations in the world. Amazon revenues in September 2023 for the 12-month period topped $638 Billion representing an 11% increase over the prior 12-month period. I remember when Amazon operated out of a garage as an online book store. The quality in the manner in which you serve people matters.

We believe that three possibilities are foundational to your thought process as you now think about the possibilities. The possibilities that you will end up thinking about will far exceed the three that we share. **Focusing on the quality of your serving effort will:**

1. **Increase effectiveness** in attracting and recruiting more people to your audience (clients, customers, members, and

brand partners). This applies to the individual entrepreneurial effort, the small and large business, and the organization.

2. **Increase the satisfaction** score of the audience you are attracting and engaging. Happy people are more productive.

3. **Increase the Lifetime Value (LTV)** of the people in your audience. Happy and satisfied people stay longer, consequently their performance may get better therefore they become more valuable as the revenues they contribute or influence grow. Happy and satisfied members contribute a rather specific amount of time or money to the endeavor. The longer they stay, the chances increase as to how much time they will invest or how much money they will give. Cultivating LTV is cost effective.

Outlook/Summary

We predict that the quality of effort focused on "serving" will become more important than the product or service provided. This is not meant to imply that a unique and distinctive product or service will not have a competitive advantage in the marketplace. We know that uniqueness has enormous appeal when marketed effectively. However, good products can also compete when great service is provided to the consumers who purchase and continue to purchase. Lifetime customer vale is a real metric and the way to increase the value of such a metric is to provide service that the customer wants to experience again and again. You, like I, have experienced many situations whereas the excellent product was not considered to be worth the investment of time and money because the value of the engagement did not meet expectations. This is true for the product we purchased, the opportunity we embraced and the organization we chose not to continue affiliation.

The opportunity for established and contemporary brands, enterprises large and small, and organizations, is not only in identifying the right channel of distribution but also how best to serve with distinction. In order to serve with distinction, a clearly defined purpose related to how best to serve the consumer and the member, within specific timeframes, will support success and sustainable success based upon growth as the most important key performance indicator.

Stats and facts serve to inform and inspire regardless of how they may sound. Whenever I have encountered a business or organization that struggles, I have also found a rather strong aversion to stats and facts, especially when the business or organization is more mature. There is an average lifespan for both business and organization. While we do not want to be a part of averages, it is good to be aware.

Standard and Poor has published the average lifespan of a company to be 21 years. Others have estimated that 30% of non-profits will fail to exist after 10 years and half fail sooner due to leadership issues and the lack of a strategic plan. I found this information by simply doing a Google and Bing search because I wanted to know. I have learned over many years to operate with a sense of urgency as I never know how much time we really have to achieve our objectives. Having a sense of urgency is considered an asset. Consistent progress and growth in returning value through serving the audience will be of paramount importance in the *NEW ECONOMY*.

CHAPTER 6

POSITIVE TRENDS FOR ALL WORKERS SEEKING MORE CONTROL, FLEXIBILITY & FREEDOM

The gig economy continues to thrive. This could be the freshman class of new individual entrepreneurs who seek flexibility and freedom in how work can be accomplished. Direct selling is expected to thrive in this unique environment because of its attributes and ability to be complimentary to core income earning via a job or any other type of income earning possibility.

There are many subsets of opportunities in the gig focused, digital platform supported economy where consumers have easier access to products, services, and the best customer service possibilities we have ever experienced. From the perspective of income earning potential, there are more choices than ever. Never in our history has it been easier to become an intermediary who helps to connect products and services with consumers and clients who need those products and services and be paid for involvement. These intermediaries and independent entrepreneurs are their own boss, and they own the investment of time and experience applied to what they choose to do. They are enabled by technology through state-of-the-art digital platforms and apps.

At the forefront of the *NEW ECONOMY* is a new type of worker. The worker who seeks and finds flexibility and freedom in how the work can be accomplished. When we wrote the book, *Ultimate Gig* (available through Amazon and others - www.ultimategigresources.com), we collaborated with many great thinkers on the subject of the gig economy to better understand the transformation of work from the rigidity of the industrial focused economy where traditional work hours became the norm to a more flexible economy where workers have more freedom to choose how, when, and where they work. We searched the research, read many books and articles, studied, and applied insightful thinking collected from a diverse group of contributors, and we conducted primary research.

A new economy has emerged. "*Fortune*'s new 50 Best Workplaces for Flexibility list actually supports the hypothesis of a *NEW ECONOMY* emerging. Many companies offer flexible work options, and their employees do get to reap the benefits. Of the 50 best companies for work flexibility on the list, 92–94% offer flex and telecommuting options. A whopping 77% of employees do take advantage of flextime, and slightly less than half (49%) telecommute. That's why nine out of ten employees report plans to grow with their companies for a long time. And workers, grateful for the flex, report that the overwhelming majority (95%) will do extra if it means getting the job done."

Technology has also enabled the reduction of risk as large investments in physical assets such as inventory are generally eliminated. This allows for more exploration by all who seek to enhance income through pursuit of flexibility and freedom in how work can be accomplished. Easy engagement and simplicity in how work can be done is essential.

We See 7 Major Trends to Watch

1. Discussions between regulators, firms, and workers as to how gig workers are to be classified and defined (independent contractor vs employee) will continue.

2. The gig economy will continue to grow and become more appealing to those who seek flexibility and freedom in how underutilized time, experience, assets, skills, and knowledge can be converted into income earning opportunities.

3. The percentage of gig workers working multiple gigs will continue to grow creating a new freshman class of micro entrepreneurs.

4. The satisfaction rate amongst gig workers is expected to remain high because gig workers learn more about themselves, enjoy what they do, gain confidence from the learning experience, and grow in confidence as to what it really means to enjoy the attribute of flexibility and freedom as to how income can be earned. This satisfaction rate is forecasted to continue to be high because the experience matches expectations, and they are realistically achievable.

5. Direct sellers will grow as a percentage of overall gig workers as direct selling companies reduce some of the complexity associated with some current direct selling models; making it easier to understand key attributes such as the ability to leverage customer acquisition, retention, and rewards from the continuous purchasing of customers and sharing with

others how they too can benefit from engagement as an intermediary.

6. Less will become more!

7. Principles and non-compromising values focused on serving the marketplace of consumers and income opportunity seekers will shape the narrative. The growth of gig workers and independent entrepreneurs will continue. The Compound Annual Growth Rate (CAGR) of participants is now forecasted to be 16%+ through 2034.

Insights/Rationale/Impact for Each Trend We Have Described

1. The debates and discussions will continue because governments depend on the collection of taxes to generate the revenue needed to serve communities. Part-time workers, those who work less than 30 hours per week have never received benefits therefore, the issue of tax compliance is the greater concern. Independent contractors can be encouraged to be compliant with rules and regulations no differently than an employee is encouraged to show up for work on time.

2. The gig economy will continue to grow because regular wages are not outpacing inflation enough. The average wage increases run consistently between 3-5% and the rate of inflation remains close nullifying any real increase in purchasing power. A flexible gig can add incremental income to household income and represent the equivalent of increased wages.

3. The percentage of gig workers working multiple gigs will continue to grow because the choices and possibilities enable working more than one gig when gigs do not conflict with one another. Developing more than one income

possibility makes sense when it is possible. Those who leverage underutilized assets, in whatever form they may be, are the new independent entrepreneurs in the *NEW ECONOMY.*

4. The satisfaction rate amongst gig workers remains high because gig workers experience realities (outcomes) that match expectations. The positioning of "gig work" by the companies providing "gig opportunities" tends to be an extremely easy to understand value proposition…immediate income possibilities that start with the possibilities of earning a few hundred dollars in accordance to time invested, not a new career. When outcomes match expectations, positioning and strategic clarity becomes easier to execute by the company and easier to understand by the worker.

5. Direct sellers will grow as a percentage of gig workers and gain more market share because it simply makes sense. Direct selling is a channel of distribution that enables intermediaries the opportunity to add value to the customer acquisition/retention process by paying a commission to the intermediary on the ongoing purchases of customers they influence directly and often indirectly. Most gig opportunities pay for the transaction one time. Direct selling companies will seize the narrative and reshape the conversation thus redefining direct selling, eliminating susceptibility to the definition's others may perceive or create.

6. *Less is more,* is not only a philosophy advocated originally by the architect Mies van der Rohe. The phrase has become a strategic imperative adopted by all businesses as we learn to do more with less. Technology is the great enabler, and this new business philosophy has made space travel simpler, the ordering of a product or service simpler and the way we work, earn incomes, and balance our lives, simpler. Complexity is an obstacle and barrier to greater marketplace engagement. In fact, we no longer tolerate

complexity. When we find complexity, we immediately move to find simplicity.

7. A focus on principles, uncompromising values, and high ethical standards, will shape the narrative and define the direct selling position in the current and future marketplace. Greater market share will be the result of clarity and speed in taking the steps to serve the marketplace in all of its formats – consumer and business model, small or large business, intermediary/worker/member/independent entrepreneur.

Insight

As we experience greater clarity through simplified business models which attract and engage people from all walks of life based upon their "purpose" with an opportunity to participate as they desire, we will also experience greater collaboration between public policy makers and those who seek more flexibility and freedom in how we can work and compliment core ways to work and build careers.

The *NEW ECONOMY* is engaging and energizing more people who own the work (in whole or in part), who will share their love for the products, services, and opportunities they represent. **"Love what you do and do what you love."**

PERSPECTIVE #1
Traditional Educational Institutions Will No Longer Be Traditional

It has become obvious to you, the reader, that we are believers and advocates of a strong trend toward the growth of entrepreneurship, especially individual entrepreneurship. When we use the term individual entrepreneur, we are also including in our mindset the independent worker in any format. All independent workers (1099 status) represent a desire to be more in control of the manner in which work can be conducted. Many are also in such status to create their own bridge between a former and new form of traditional employment.

In my interactions with Dr. Peterson, he has often asked the question: Who is going to train this new type of worker? The question is actually a brilliant one. The answer requires reflection on how the training of independent workers might be approached and how our traditional educational formats will react to the emergence of what we describe as a *NEW ECONOMY*. Ironically, independent workers are described as those who do not receive traditional employee types of support so providing benefits of any type to independent workers has always been prohibited by both federal and local government. Training cannot be mandatory therefore, any guidance provided must be in the category of being voluntary. Remember, the "independent worker/entrepreneur" is not an employee.

New resources will emerge to support the trends toward a *NEW ECONOMY* and there are many such products, services and support emerging,… many are discussed in this book in Chapter 11. However, traditional educational resources are impacted as well. Contemporary trends always mean that something that has been existing is probably forced to change otherwise, it no longer remains relevant.

I remember reading a news bulletin in "Morning Brew" a daily online newsletter that stated: An estimated 40% of this year's college graduates may never work a traditional job! This created a big WOW in my mindset. I was not as interested in tracking down the validity of the statement as much as I was interested in the thoughts that were triggered. Our group has never explored research into the state of our educational institutions; however, it is very easy to observe that education - both secondary, post-secondary, as well as graduate level, have transformed and evolved. The physical building(s) are no longer requisite to obtaining an education. The

University of Phoenix may be recognized as the pioneer of online/ affordable post-secondary educational opportunities; however, no post-secondary educational institution can remain totally reliant upon campus classes… at least from our perspective. The University of Maryland is now recognized as a global institution because of its effectiveness in delivering online education. The enrollment at the University of Phoenix is reported to have been in excess of 100,000 at the end of 2024.

The preceding is offered as a perspective and also a realization that we no longer have excuses for not pursuing as much education as possible. What was once unaffordable for many can now be affordable to the masses. Personally, I have completed a couple of online degree programs, not for the credentials but for the stimulation of mindset, the ability to increase my problem-solving capacity, effectiveness, and, … of course, to remain coordinated in support of my lifelong commitment to continuous study and learning.

Therefore, in the *NEW ECONOMY*, we envision a much flatter playing field whereas new EQUALIZERS will equip more of the masses. Our educational possibilities will emerge in newer and relevant formats, and we are already experiencing these possibilities. We predict that post-secondary education will shift to be more inclusive of the possibility that 50% of graduates may never work a traditional job as we have defined jobs and careers over the past 50 years. We also envision the Business School curricular to continue to shift toward the new reality, … more and more students may be in the business school to become better equipped to become successful entrepreneurial leaders vs engagement of a traditional job with a major brand/corporation. A few of our most successful corporations today were created by founders who envisioned their idea, and how they might execute the idea, before they finished their post-secondary/graduate school experience.

Our definition of education will continue to transform and evolve in the *NEW ECONOMY*!

PERSPECTIVE #2
Women Are Empowered

The story relative to the phenomenal growth of gig economy participation continues to be a story about the growth in the participation of women. When we first started our formal observations of the gig economy, the rate of participation for women was approximately 33%. Today, the rate of participation is viewed to be about equal to that of men and growing.

Why are so many women attracted to gig work? Well, the traditional job market remains dominated by men. Women appear to appreciate flexibility and certainly desire wage equality. While there has been substantial progress over the past 100 years, wage inequality continues to exist, especially in the higher paying traditional jobs. Women continue to bravely fight this battle on all fronts, and some are finding the gig economy to be the ultimate equalizer.

When it comes to choosing a gig, certain types of opportunities are more appealing to women than men and vice versa. Women have historically represented the higher percentage of direct sellers (75% to 25%), and we do not envision much change as a percentage of participants in a direct selling opportunity. Obviously, some direct selling companies will be more favorable to men because of the products or services being sold; however, overall ... the future of the *NEW ECONOMY* appears to be very inclusive of women in many new ways as the *NEW ECONOMY* represents the greatest transfer of work ownership in the last 100 years. The work can now be owned by the Independent worker (a portion of the work, significant percentage if not 100%) who is also becoming the new form of independent entrepreneur, and women will play many roles.

This perspective was also shared in *Ultimate Gig*. Below are highlights of the same five reasons, first shared in *Ultimate Gig*, as to why we continue to foresee women continuing to play greater and greater roles in the *NEW ECONOMY.*

1. **Women appreciate flexibility and freedom in how work can be done.** The *NEW ECONOMY* offers many attributes and many choices. Gigs may not be the ideal solution in all cases, but women will recognize and appreciate the options. Gig work provides a path to juggling rewarding work with childcare, eldercare, and household responsibilities that fall disproportionately to women. Gigs making effective use of technology have made it possible for flexible work to be efficient, in some cases providing earning opportunities without leaving home.

   Part of the flexibility of gigs and *NEW ECONOMY* opportunities and possibilities is that these can be short-term work arrangements. People can take on "new work" when it fits their schedule, and they are free to stop and start that schedule as they choose, without jeopardizing a relationship with an employer. The gig economy has completely redefined part-time work and created independent entrepreneurial opportunities favorable to women who desire to work on their own schedules.

2. *NEW ECONOMY* **Opportunities offer an alternative to trying to break the glass ceiling.** The new opportunities and possibilities do not include the traditional organizational structure of a "boss" who manages the worker. There is no boss and typically no organizational politics. Gig workers usually are not competing with others to get the same job or the same promotion. In the *NEW ECONOMY*, the gig participant is her own boss, certainly a refreshing option that eliminates many of the challenges women have been fighting in the workplace for many years. Flexibility and freedom in how work can be done also removes age as a barrier to obtaining work and the challenges associated with re-entry to the work world for those who have stepped away.

3. **Women appear to appreciate *Work From Home Possibilities.*** Working women often continue to shoulder the majority of childcare, education of the children and sometimes the responsibilities associated with elderly care of family members. Being forced to work from home during the years of the pandemic may have accelerated the preference to work from home, making gigs *NEW ECONOMY* work even more appealing to women.

4. **Gender equality may be another hidden benefit of working a gig.** Many gig participants market their services with company support or digital formats that do not reveal the gender of the worker. Therefore, customers make their choices based on what they see (the product or service), not who is providing the product or service. This is another asset that the gig economy offers, perhaps without even realizing it.

   In fact, gig economy opportunities may be eliminating gender inequality. The following is a great study: *The 2018 APAC Workforce Insights Study, Gig Economy: How Free Agents are redefining work, the closing of the inequality of pay gap relative to gender.* In traditional jobs, the difference in pay between men and women is about 12% (favorable to men); however, the gig economy appears to be less, maybe as low as 5%.

5. ***"The Artificial Intelligence (AI) revolution is upon us, poised to revolutionize the world of work in ways beyond our current comprehension. From finance to healthcare, manufacturing to media, its impact is already being felt across various sectors, compelling businesses of all sizes to adapt swiftly. From restructuring workflows to upskilling employees, evolution is not just a necessity but a strategic necessity in navigating the shifting employment terrain."*** www.BTIexecutivesearch.com

In our reading and study, we found the above quote from an executive search firm in Asia focused on helping clients in Asia find their most valuable asset: the right **PEOPLE**. *"We firmly believe that it's through the right people that teams are able to maximize their potential and create value for their organizations."*

The quote that we share is a reminder of the powerful role artificial intelligence will play in all work-related activities. The impact is global.

Women working from home in a flexible manner, freelancer, consultant, educator, independent entrepreneur of any type, will benefit as the need for advice, more skill sets, will be available through artificial intelligence. Both men and women working in a flexible type of work are expected to benefit.

6. **Quick payment for services rendered.** Quicker pay is an attribute of most gigs and is considered to be a short-term motivation that women may have for seeking a gig. Gig-providing companies were among the first to offer a more immediate compensation opportunity paying the gig worker almost immediately for services performed. This attribute associated with the attribute of flexibility and the many forms of gig work choices is appealing.

7. **Short-term work opportunities are appealing.** Many women are not seeking long-term employment but would enjoy meaningful, short-term work. Part-time jobs satisfied this need and desire at one time; however, the gig economy has completed redefined part-time work and created micro-entrepreneurial opportunities favorable to women who desire to work on their own schedules. There are both more types of part-time work and more opportunities available in the gig economy than ever before.

The *NEW ECONOMY* is empowering. Both men and women will benefit enormously.

PROSPECTIVE #3
Why Entrepreneurship Is
Worth Exploring!

When reflecting on any conversations in local and national media relative to the accuracy of "Job" reporting, it becomes rather obvious that the more important statistic may be related to the satisfaction of the people, the people who continue to seek: Work, stability in income being earned, along with a personal definition of success. Regardless of the number of jobs created or lost; Are we happier overall, more confident in our ability to make the "Life/Work" equation work better? This is an important question to ask oneself, especially during a time whereas innovation and technological advancements are leading us into a *NEW ECONOMY* where we can do more with less.

The emergence of "artificial intelligence" will enhance productivity and, according to most predictions, replace or displace many people working traditional jobs. The questions are many and the number of traditional jobs should be expected to decrease when making comparisons to historical metrics. A conversation about the new opportunities and possibilities may be the more important conversation.

What matters most...the number of jobs created, or the number of opportunities created for people from all walks of life regardless of age, past experience, or inexperience? The BLS data must be viewed in detail. Reporting the number of workers, new or existing, who are in W-2 status (traditional employees) is a much easier number to report vs the number of new people entering independent contractor or 1099 status.

The gig economy has opened many new doors of opportunity and possibility. The gig economy is not an economy of new part time workers. The gig economy is actually at the foundation of a *NEW ECONOMY* where more flexibility and freedom in how we can work and leverage underutilized assets is a possibility. The underutilized assets can be in the form of time, experience, skills, knowledge, passion, and/or purpose. Age is not a factor or barrier.

All jobs require a certain skill set, often a level of experience, and certain age groups are always included or excluded. The preceding is not true in the *NEW ECONOMY* whereas the gig economy is foundational. **The job reports that we tend to hear about do not include the number of independent contractors and/or 1099 workers who have recently become engaged.**

For those working remotely in a traditional job structure, there is more freedom and flexibility associated with how the work is performed. Regular connection with the company, and teams within the company, are required. However, much of the work is accomplished at times whereas the worker can also address other priorities such as family, additional income possibilities, and study.

Based upon personal research and study, more workers will explore the possibility of being an Independent Entrepreneur in some form. There is also a growing debate in the corporate sector as to the value of extending flexibility to workers or returning to the more comfortable and rigid format of traditional working hours of 9 to 5, five days per week. These debates are more likely to fuel the fires of entrepreneurship in their many new formats vs settle the argument or justify any corporate position.

The facts: Flexibility and freedom in how work can be done is growing in popularity. The gig economy is proof of concept. The growth rate in gig work participation continues to be at an annual compound growth rate that is estimated to be around 16% through 2034 (Gig Economy Market Size & Share 2034).

In summary: Flexibility and freedom are expected to become more important in our plans for how we pursue the work/life relationship over the coming years. As people from all walks of life embrace, struggle with, and adapt to change, possible replacement or displacement due to advancements in technology, we are expected to continue to evolve in how we think, what we value, and ultimately...how we work. The facts are: More can be accomplished with less; however, the value of human contribution has been fundamental to progress in societies and cultures since the beginning of recorded history. We should not expect this to change. There are ongoing changes in just about everything that we do.

This moment in time has been coming for several years. Fifteen to twenty years ago, it is doubtful that we would have thought of the attorney who never works in an office or the medical student who never practices in an official capacity within an office or hospital. We knew of those who did babysitting or elderly care for what we termed "extra income." Today, dog walking has become a profitable enterprise for a solopreneur/gig worker. A Task Rabbit can be hired to do almost anything that we would not want to do ourselves. Hobbies have become businesses due to the availability of the internet as a tool of commerce. Upwork is a proven concept and model that connects talent, skill and experience with another entity which needs the resource and neither needs to be in the same geography or time zone.

From the highly skilled to the unskilled, opportunities to more effectively leverage assets now exist and these opportunities are available to the masses, not simply a select few.

From this perspective, based upon personal reading, study and observation, the exploration of solopreneur opportunities is a wise investment of time. The opportunities and possibilities are actually unlimited, and new possibilities are being invented as we author this article.

From personal perspective and experience, direct selling opportunities are, perhaps, best positioned to be at the top of any list of opportunities and possibilities to explore. There are some very specific reasons for this recommendation which are beyond the personal bias of being an advocate. Direct selling opportunities are:

1. Easy to engage

2. Easy to align passion, purpose, and personal values

3. Easy to share with others who become customers and advocates of the brand themselves.

I am not assuming that all direct selling companies have or will achieve clarity in their strategies to attract a sizable portion of the marketplace. This is that moment in time whereas companies embracing a direct selling channel of distribution have the opportunity to survive and thrive in the *NEW ECONOMY* whereas flexibility and freedom in how work can be accomplished is no longer a "nice to have" but for many, a "must have!" We know that the ability to create multiple income streams is growing in popularity (60% of gig workers were found to be working multiple gigs – Fleming, Peterson, *Ultimate Gig* research 2023.

The direct selling model of engaging people from all walks of life to be the energy behind the distribution of products and services certainly are in a position to be recognized as the most relevant of opportunities and possibilities. Labels and definitions of what direct selling actually means will change. The changes, whatever they may be, provide opportunities to demonstrate a greater degree of relevance to marketplace behaviors and perceived needs.

PERSPECTIVE #4
Safety Nets Are Available To *New Economy* Independent Workers

As our current economy moves from the more traditional and structured approach of how people engage work to a more flexible approach whereas the worker even owns a portion of the work, workers will not be eligible for traditional benefits offered by traditional employers. via their independent contractor status. Some public policy advisors will continue to be concerned. One of their primary objectives is to protect workers from misuse of the services they provide to those who seek those services. The collection of taxes and adherence to rules of law are more difficult to control with independent workers vs those who are traditional employees.

We remind all that America was built on the work efforts of those who were entrepreneurial. Entrepreneurs have always chosen to accept certain risks that others would not in exchange for the opportunity to bring innovation and often transformation into society. Entrepreneurs have always needed basic support to do what they do. Financial assistance and various forms of insurance products along with access to news, information, education, and supportive services to compliment the new efforts of the entrepreneur have always been needed, and entrepreneurs have always found a way to access those services.

From our perspective, at this time, the *NEW ECONOMY* will be an economy of independent entrepreneurs. New safety nets are already emerging in many different formats. Employee benefits associated with the traditional job will remain an asset when engaged in traditional forms of employment. *NEW ECONOMY* entrepreneurs will have access to products and services of a vast variety. Most important to the independent entrepreneur is simply the opportunity to access diverse types of products and services that fill their specific needs.

In the closing chapter of this book, we recommend a few essential products/services designed with contemporary features which support a *NEW ECONOMY* worker/entrepreneur.

CHAPTER 7
EXPLORING DIRECT SELLING IS ENCOURAGED

M y academic friends always refer to direct selling as a channel of distribution. After many years of observation, research and study of business models, possibilities and opportunities whereas "people" can engage without typical restrictions be it the resume, age, skill level, past experience or inexperience, I found direct selling companies to offer what might be considered a dream come true for some, the ultimate gig for others and the ideal pathway to independent entrepreneurship.

Basic Stats and Facts About Direct Selling in the United States

U.S. Direct Selling	Retail Sales & Participants
Sales	$33 Billion
Services	34%
Health/Wellness	32%
Home & Family	16%
Personal Care	10%
Clothing/Accessories	5%
Leisure & Education	3%
Direct Sellers	6.1 Million
Full Time	0.5 Million
Part Time	5.6 Million
Women	74%
Men	26%
Preferred Customers/Discount Buyers	38 Million

Note: The data in the previous chart is sourced from the U.S. Direct Selling Association. The data represents 2023 performance in the United States. All retail sales data is rounded up.

Direct selling companies grow their channel of distribution by offering people the opportunity to become intermediaries who represent the brand, acquire customers and other brand partners who will also expand the channel of distribution. This model is very different from the basic gig model, models of franchising or expanding through more and more retail outlets that are physical in nature. Direct selling companies are also using their digital platforms effectively to keep their brands and brand partners supported 24/7, realizing that consumers now shop eCommerce platforms at any time from anyplace.

Direct Selling Companies Embrace eCommerce

We offer the following articles as resources which document the incredible impact of eCommerce on the marketplace of consumers and business models of all types.

In 2025, global e-commerce sales are projected to exceed **4.3 trillion U.S. dollars**, with a **CAGR of 5.34%** from 2025 to 2030.

• In the U.S., e-commerce sales are expected to total **$1.47 trillion** in 2025, reflecting a **9.78% increase** from 2024.

• Year-over-year growth is crucial for e-commerce businesses, as it helps track trends, assess market position, and align strategies with long-term objectives.

Direct Selling – Origins and Evolution

Over the past 100 years, the direct selling channel of distribution has evolved along a similar pathway to what we now refer to as the traditional industrial economy business model which is also over 100 years old.

The origins of the direct selling model include those periods whereas direct sellers sold "door to door" in neighborhoods across the country. Today, those who sell products or services door to door are probably zero. The direct selling model evolved to what was referred to as the "party plan" or "group selling" method where groups gathered, primarily in the home of a host, to witness demonstrations and enjoy personalized conversations about a product or service.

Today, we no longer debate the fact that we have evolved through the agricultural revolution, industrial revolution, technological revolution to what is now referred to as multiple revolutions – traditional commerce dependent upon physical interaction and exchange to ecommerce which requires no physical interaction, commerce to ecommerce, physical to digital…to work which now embraces flexibility and freedom of choice more so than at any other time in the history of our civilized society. The direct selling business model has also evolved.

Our most recent research has uncovered broad trends that may portend the future of the gig economy; these trends have specific implications for those using the direct selling channel of distribution and the direct sellers who choose a direct selling company.

Amazon has proven that excellence in customer service attracts and retains customers. Amazon and others are also proof of concept that ecommerce is real, and products and services can be engaged without physical presence being a prerequisite. Today's direct selling companies capitalize on the learning and experiences of other business models that have changed the game with innovative technology, excellent digital platforms, outstanding customer service, and innovative contemporary tools to support the direct sellers who engage a company/brand.

Author's Personal Perspective

When I reflect on how I got involved in direct selling, it amazes me even to this day, because it was so "out of character" for me. I was committed to a career in the field of architecture and working in an office which included the best of architectural thought leaders. However, I was also experiencing the responsibility of marriage and the possibilities of family life. Money, or the lack of money, became a dilemma. I wanted to pay the bills, but the month kept running out before I could complete the process. My wife's first cousin, who I met in architectural school, had introduced me to my wife. He also introduced me to a gentleman – an educator and believer in big dreams, who later became a best friend and the godfather of our second child. Our friendship transcended into brotherhood. Mr. Willie Larkin introduced me to the concept of direct selling, where I would ultimately learn more about myself than I had learned in college. The experience was absolutely incredible.

It was Mr. Larkin who sensed my goal in my life to be a relevant husband and father - pay the bills and have enough left to manage a family successfully. Marriage changed the game. I was proud of what I was accomplishing in the field of architecture, but I knew that I had not achieved what I envisioned as success. Our first child, Kassandra, added both joy and additional responsibilities as we were now parents. We were blessed with a son, John III, who was born about 4 years later. We continued to learn more about our lives, our work, and what mattered most.

Mr. Larkin had faced the same challenges as a dedicated educator, teaching in the school system in Chicago. He and his wife Versie had four children. However, Mr. Larkin never let any circumstances limit his belief in possibilities. He believed that there was always a better pathway for someone who is relevant, and he used that determination to gain part-time shift work as a Chicago bus driver after a full day of teaching school. He had a purpose: to provide for his family in more than an ordinary fashion. Mr. Larkin found direct selling, and he shared what he had found with me. He loved the idea of representing **a brand of products that people could purchase only from, or through, an independent direct seller.**

Prior to meeting Mr. Larkin, my understanding of direct selling was very limited. I knew Avon was referred to as a direct selling company and that was about the extent of my knowledge. I did not really understand the significance of how a direct selling business model actually worked. Even though I had an interest and need to earn more money, I was attracted to direct selling for other reasons that were important to us. **The idea of "ownership" of an activity associated with an established brand was the primary motivator.** Although I needed to earn additional income at that time, I was not interested in chasing dollars. My time was precious, and I knew that I had to find something that I would love to do, ... and if I did, I would love to do it often.

My wife Joyce and I learned to work our direct selling business together. I was totally amazed at how a channel of distribution could attract people from all walks of life to the personal selling of products and services. In the beginning, it made little sense to my architectural mindset; however, as time elapsed, Joyce and I learned to focus on basics associated with principles and values, and most importantly - the people who became customers and independent direct sellers themselves. We witnessed how the business model could easily be abused by those with a "money focused" mentality. Our experiences were always based upon our beliefs in the products, opportunity, and company. The company's principles and values were always very important to us.

Mr. Larkin taught us that money is a result of actions, our performance, and the value we extend to others. His philosophies and beliefs made a lot of sense. We learned a lot in our early days of direct selling. Because we kept learning we realized how relevant it was to earn a few hundred dollars per month incremental to what we already earned. We watched many people "quit" their venture into direct selling before they ever got started because they thought they could simply recruit others to do something they were not doing themselves. They focused on what "could" be created "if" they "could" build an organization of direct sellers directly and indirectly. In other words, so many who quit before they ever got started simply thought that they could recruit others to do something that they were not doing themselves. **Direct selling does not work that way from this perspective.**

Our approach to building an income from direct selling involvement was different. I never thought that anything worthwhile could be gained quickly even though we needed to earn more income as quickly as possible. Selling/Sharing the products we were affiliated with just made sense because we believed in them, and they worked for us, and we could earn commissions on the purchases made by new customers who we influenced. We always thought of our involvement as being one of sharing with others something we believed in ourselves. We never embraced the word "selling" or even "recruiting" because words can influence mindset. Therefore, conducting parties/home shows/group meetings always appeared to be both efficient and effective. From time to time, we jumped on planes and trains and drove to a lot to meetings, wherever they were or wherever we could schedule time with someone else. Our telephone bill also went up, not down, when we were trying to reduce expenses because expenses were exceeding income. We were not examples of "quick success" if there is any such thing. We succeeded because of our passion and advocacy of what we believed in. Over a period of a few years, we avoided any disruption to our core income and actually replaced three jobs. My wife was working in two of those jobs. Our biggest challenge, which I had to overcome, was my personal mindset at that time. My dream was to be an architect, not a direct seller!

Today, there is no need to do all of what we did to build our direct selling business because the selling/sharing process is very different. Technology provides tools, whereas we can connect with people virtually with no geographical or time zone constraints and still add a personalized touch to the conversations which are more focused on sharing vs selling.

Our first direct selling company went out of business. The new owners reorganized, and I was asked to play a key role, so I did. After a few years, along with a few friends, I bought the company. Years later, I merged with another direct selling company. By then I had become involved with the *U.S. Direct Selling Association*. Once I committed to the direct selling business model, my primary objective was to always meet and associate, as best I could, with those identified as legendary direct sellers. I met a few, including Bob King, Mary Kay, Mary Crowley, Rich DeVos, Erik Lane, Jim Preston, Rick Goings, and many others. Through association and interaction with others who I held in "legendary" category, I became convinced that I would always strive to remain relevant within the direct selling space by continuing to grow and learn. Becoming the architect of one's own destiny and helping others learn what the phrase meant, now became more important to me than being an architect of building design.

Even though I was now becoming a believer and advocate of the direct selling model, my foundational commitments to being relevant were simply transferred. The principles that I had learned relating to the design and construction of buildings remained integral to my core philosophical beliefs. I now wanted to be relevant as a direct selling executive.

Direct Sellers Manage the Primary Responsibility of Acquiring, Engaging, and Retaining Customers by Adding Value

Popular gig work, which rewards for performing a specific task at a specific time, does not generally offer an opportunity to benefit from future or repetitive purchases. A direct seller can expect the possibility of a continuous relationship with the customer who makes a purchase of the product or service the direct seller initiated. This possibility activates a residual income. The cost of customer acquisition requires an investment of time therefore the *Return On Work Effort* (ROWE) may increase as the effort of customer retention is usually impacted by customer belief in the value of the brand and service they engage in. This attribute makes direct selling complimentary to almost any other core income earning opportunity, even other gig work.

A direct seller is an independent contractor who engages with a direct selling company. The direct selling company is building a brand of products and/or services and markets the products or services to consumers through intermediaries – the direct seller. The direct seller benefits from the relationship by adding an individualized touch to the marketing and selling of the products or services using approved tools generally provided by the company. Direct sellers not only benefit from customer acquisition and retention they benefit from the initial purchase by the customer and ongoing purchases the customer may make. In essence, the direct seller owns

a part of the customer relationship as long as they are active and effective in adding value to the relationship with the customer.

Direct Sellers Are Also Rewarded for Duplicating Their Behaviors.

Every direct seller is actually a new channel of distribution for the direct selling company. When direct sellers themselves provide others with the opportunity to create their own channel of distribution, the original direct seller typically expands their income potential.

The preceding is a powerful attribute of a direct selling opportunity as it emulates the duplication effort that franchising has utilized to create some of the largest and most notable brands in the world. Direct selling opportunities are similar to franchise opportunities in many ways without the risk or investment associated with the franchise model. **Most notable about direct selling is the opportunity to advocate for a brand and benefit from the new customers and brand partners, attracted by the direct seller, who also engage the brand.**

We Offer the Following Guide When Exploring Direct Selling

1. **Search and choose** a company that represents a product or service which aligns with your beliefs, personal principles and values, passion, and purpose. When you love the product or service you can easily share the product or service with others.

2. **Seek simplicity and clarity** in what the direct selling company provides. Engagement should be easy to understand and very affordable.

3. **Review the tools and guidelines** the company will provide and the help/support that you might receive from an individual who will sponsor you into the direct selling company. They should already be building their own direct selling business enabling you to benefit from their experience. Their experience should not be hypothetical.

Direct selling companies typically have unique approaches to how compensation will be paid for performance. Be careful when reviewing "what if you do this or that" scenarios. Direct selling rewards you for what you do when you do it. Here is what you can expect to do as a direct seller:

1. **Be your own best customer.**

2. **Share with others what was shared with you.**

3. **Show others how to do what you are learning to do.**

Personal Reflection: Because we had an excellent sponsor when my wife and I chose our direct selling experience, we quickly understood the value of the customer. Because we absolutely loved and believed in the products, we were our own best customers, and we looked forward to sharing with others what we had found. All businesses are based upon customers and clients. We quickly realized that having 10 to 12 personal customers would be essential for any direct seller's business, so we aimed to acquire many customers as quickly as possible. We acquired many. Through our personal conversations and group interactions, we simply shared our love.

As others became customers, we became more and more excited and many of our new customers wanted to do what we were doing. Building our direct selling business was so much fun! Sure enough, many of our new brand partners (they were referred to as distributors in those days) came from our new bevy of customers. Guess what! The products we were so excited about were biodegradable cleaning products which we enthusiastically shared with others. Others also felt our passion and purpose! We were simply intrigued by products that did not contribute to the pollution of our planet.

I am willing, from personal experience, to assert the following: ***When you love the product or service, you will share that experience with others authentically, and others will want to do what you are doing because it appears to be an enjoyable activity.***

My wife and I always understood that we could only build a business by being an example to others as to what might be possible.

Here Is What Might Be Possible...Realistically

1. **Twelve or more personally purchasing customers**, within a reasonable time frame, will result in customer purchases exceeding $1,000.00 when the average order is approximately $80.00. You will earn approximately $200.00 in most direct selling companies. The time frame might be a week, month, or quarter, you control the work effort and performance.

2. **When you personally duplicate your behavior into 12 others** who do the same thing that you have done, you will probably be rewarded for the behaviors that you have duplicated into others. Your additional income earned should approach $1,000.00 whenever the cumulative efforts occur within a specific timeframe – week, month, or quarter. Once again, the work effort and performance is controlled by you and those whom you have shared.

3. **When** a service focused direct selling company becomes your choice, the average order per customer will most likely be greater and so will your income potential from customers purchasing directly and indirectly.

Note: As with the selection of any income possibility, it is important to seek clarity and understanding relative to the work effort/performance/behavior required to be compensated. Make your selections based upon what you know you will love to do, and you will do what you love to do effectively and consistently. Therefore, you can expect to get better and better at what you are doing.

Direct selling possibilities and opportunities, from personal perspective, should be explored. Regardless of what else you may be involved in, the products and services created and marketed by direct selling companies are typically unique and of very high quality. I love the supplements that I use because they are not marketed for mass market appeal. They are designed for those who desire to supplement their nutritional intake with quality supplements and optimizers. I do not put cheap gas in my car. I consider the quality of what I put into my body to be more important, therefore I consider the fuel for my body, and the supplements that I select, to be very important.

You too can find that product or service that activates your passions, your purpose, your love, and advocacy. Who would ever have thought that someone who spent most of his childhood years dreaming of becoming an architect would fall in love with biodegradable cleaning products? It happened, and it has also happened to so many others representing every walk of life you can imagine. **I fell in love with a channel of distribution that attracts and supports people from all walks of life with an opportunity to participate as a brand partner, owning a part of the customer and brand partner relationship.**

Being limited to a sole source of income no longer exists. An individual's ability to increase his or her income potential is only limited by the person's objectives and the number of hours available to embrace and learn a new activity.

PROFESSIONAL AND PERSONAL BENEFITS OF A DIRECT SELLING EXPERIENCE

Robert A. Perterson PHD
The University of Texas at Austin

A personal note from the author: Dr. Peterson is a personal friend and has been a mentor for many years. He has taught me the skill of "thinking" encouraging me to ask myself more questions when I thought I had answered all the questions that I needed to answer. Based upon my personal experience, and to the best of my recollection, Dr. Peterson was one of the very first distinguished professors to take a keen interest in the direct selling business model. The White Paper – Professional and Personal Benefits Of A Direct Selling Experience, created for the **U.S Direct Selling Education Foundation**, is reprinted below with slight modification. It was an extraordinary glimpse into the professional and personal benefits gained from a direct selling experience. We are proud to offer this paper in this book. The empirical research referenced in this paper was conducted by Dr. Peterson.

Direct selling is simultaneously a channel of distribution and a business model that offers entrepreneurial opportunities for individuals to market and sell products and services, typically outside of a fixed retail establishment, through one-to-one selling, in-home product demonstrations, and/or online. As a distribution channel, direct selling is ubiquitous and, touches the lives of millions of Americans. Individuals are drawn to direct selling for a multitude of reasons beyond a desire to earn a living as a full-time direct seller or to earn extra income or make a special purchase as a part-time direct seller. The research reported here documents the impact of a direct selling experience on 14 business and professional skills as well as on 13 personal life skills. **A substantial majority of the current direct sellers**

surveyed, more than three-fourths, agreed that they benefitted from their direct selling experience in terms of improved business and professional skills, and that skills gained from a direct selling experience transferred to their personal lives. Moreover, there were significant and positive relationships between self-perceived skill levels and self-perceptions of direct selling success and performance in a non-direct selling job.

Findings regarding the impact of direct selling experience on personal life skills in particular suggest that a direct selling experience can have a powerful influence beyond direct selling per se and, as such, can indirectly contribute to the betterment of society. A national sample of 495 current direct sellers and 465 former direct sellers were surveyed for this research. Findings from this research have several practical implications for recruiting, training, and retaining direct sellers. These findings and implications are briefly summarized below.

Reasons for Joining Direct Selling Company

Twelve (12) possible reasons why the direct seller's surveyed joined their current direct selling company were investigated.

The most frequently stated reason for joining a direct selling company was *"I believed that the products are of such value that I wanted to share them with my friends, neighbors, and the public."* **Eighty-one percent of the survey participants stated that this was a reason they joined their current direct selling company.** The least frequently cited reason for joining a direct selling company was "I wanted a full-time working career." In general, the reasons for joining a direct selling company can be categorized as **"people/social, financial,"** and desire for a specific **"product."** The median number of reasons survey participants gave for joining their current direct selling company was seven (7).

Reasons for Joining a Direct Selling Company

Reasons	Women	Men
Full Time Career	31%	54%
Purchase product at discount	61%	81%
Recognition for performance	57%	39%
Reasons	**Non-Millennials**	**Millennials**
Full Time Career	28%	46%
Feel at ease with public speaking	32%	56%

Insights: Of the current direct sellers surveyed regarding their reasons for joining a direct selling company: Males were more likely than females to want a full-time direct selling job. Eighty-one percent of the female direct sellers stated that they wanted to purchase their direct selling company's product(s) at a discount for themselves and/or their family versus 61% of the male direct sellers. Fifty-seven percent of the male direct sellers were interested in the recognition that they would receive for their [sales] efforts compared to 39% of the female direct sellers. Seventy-two percent of the male direct sellers were interested in enhancing their personal development (i.e., becoming more confident, better business-minded) through direct selling, whereas 53% of the female direct sellers stated such an interest.

No differences were observed regarding reasons for joining a direct selling company between urban and rural direct sellers, or among direct sellers who had been with their direct selling company for various time periods. More millennial direct sellers than non-millennials joined their current company seeking a full-time career.

Millennials also wanted to feel more at ease in front of other people relative to non-millennials.

Skill Improvements Due to
Direct Selling Experience

Professional Skill	Men	Women
Critical Thinking	88%	74%
Stress Management	85%	69%
Problem Solving	90%	76%
Public Speaking	84%	71%
Time Management	87%	77%
Entrepreneurship	90%	78%
Decision Making	87%	78%
Finance Management	83%	77%

Insights: The research examined 14 business/ professional and 13 personal life skills that might be improved or fostered by a direct selling experience. Survey participants were first asked whether they "strongly disagree," "somewhat disagree," "somewhat agree," or "strongly agree" that their direct selling experience was beneficial in terms of improving or fostering each of the 14 business/ professional skills. For example, they were asked whether they "strongly disagree," "somewhat disagree," "somewhat agree," or "strongly agree" that "I improved my decision-making skills" (as a consequence of their direct selling experience). Similarly, survey participants were asked whether they "strongly disagree," "somewhat disagree," "somewhat agree," or "strongly agree" that they had been able to transfer each of 13 skills emanating from their direct selling experience to their personal lives.

Consequently, in an absolute sense the current direct sellers surveyed believed that "lessons learned" through their direct selling experience were helpful in both their business/ professional careers and their personal lives.

Across the seven skills that were common to the business/ professional and personal life skill sets, survey participants indicated that the skills they acquired from their direct selling experience were slightly more beneficial to their personal lives than to their business/professional careers.

On average, more than 75% of direct sellers surveyed agreed that both their business/professional skill levels improved and that their personal lives benefited due to skills emanating from their direct selling experience. Even so, despite the high absolute level of overall agreement that a direct selling experience improved or fostered skill levels, perceptual differences did occur between male and female direct sellers. With respect to business/ professional skills that were believed to have been improved due to a direct selling experience, proportionally more male direct sellers than female direct sellers believed that their sales skills had improved (88% versus 77%) and that they undertook more [business-related] initiatives (87% versus 73%).

Personal Skills Believed to Have Been Improved by Direct Selling Experience

Personal Skill	Millennials	Non-Millennials
Decision Making	86%	78%
Interpersonal Relationships	87%	75%
Stress Management	81%	70%

Insight: In an absolute sense, a majority of all direct sellers studied, current as well as former, believed that both their business/ professional and personal life skills were improved by their direct selling experience.

Performance In Non-Direct Selling Jobs

Eighty percent of the survey participants who were current direct sellers stated that they also had a job other than direct selling. (This reinforces the conclusion that direct selling tends to be a part-time pursuit.) These survey participants (and former direct sellers surveyed) were asked whether they agreed or disagreed with the statement, "Because of my direct selling experience, I perform better in other, non-direct selling jobs," using a 4-category rating scale ranging from "strongly disagree" to "strongly agree."

A substantial percentage of the survey participants who were current direct sellers and who held a non-direct selling job—84%—noted improved performance due to lessons learned through their direct selling experience. As might be expected, given differences in reasons for joining a direct selling company and self-perceived skill levels between current and former direct sellers, the percentage of current sellers (84%) believing their direct selling experience helped them perform better in a non-direct selling job was significantly larger than the corresponding percentage (66%) observed for former direct sellers. Likewise, proportionally more male direct sellers (90%) than female direct sellers (80%) believed their direct selling experience helped them perform better in a non-direct selling job.

Self-perceived performance in a non-direct selling job was significantly and positively correlated with self-perceptions of direct selling success. In addition, survey participants holding a non-direct selling job also believed that skills emanating from their direct selling experience improved their performance in their non-direct selling job. Moreover, survey participants who stated that one reason for joining a direct selling company was to improve their personal development (i.e., become more confident, better business-minded) also believed that skills emanating from their direct selling experience enhanced their performance in a non-direct selling job.

In brief, individuals who experience a direct selling opportunity may gain skills that can be applied in a non-direct selling job as well as in their personal lives. Finally, each of the 27 business/professional and personal life skills studied was significantly and positively correlated with perceived performance in a non-direct selling job.

These findings highlight the transferable nature of skills developed through direct selling. Many participants reported that the communication, organization, and leadership abilities honed while working as direct sellers were directly applicable and beneficial in their professional roles.

PERSPECTIVE #1
Direct Sellers Are Entrepreneurs

Over my many years of direct and indirect involvement with the direct selling business model, I have been witness to many outstanding accomplishments that transcend the perception that many have of those who engage in incremental income earning opportunities. As you now know, my wife and I were direct sellers and eventually we became successful. My movement into the executive ranks of a direct selling company was our only reason for ceasing the efforts that we had grown to enjoy. For us to continue building our business once I became an executive was considered by us as being a "conflict of interest."

As an executive, I remained of the belief that the "heart and soul" of the direct selling business model was in the hearts and souls of those who engaged as a direct seller. From this perspective, the direct seller who engages because of their love and belief in the product or service always started their business building efforts on a firm foundation. Those who engaged for the sole purpose of attempting to earn money were more short-term participants vs those who enjoyed sharing the product or service that personally loved. The short-term participants often expressed disappointment in their earnings, and their earnings goals were, more often than not, a bit unrealistic... at least from this point-of-view.

During my experience as a direct selling executive, I developed very close and strong relationships with many direct sellers who I admired very much. Their examples often caused me to wonder if I had made the right decision in venturing into the executive ranks. I cannot mention all of those who I admire, however, I share brief stories of the following two women who are unforgettable. I will only refer to them by initials.

I met VMK during our initial experience as direct sellers. She had previous experience with a company that utilized what was called, at that time, the party plan method of selling. The party plan method was fun because during those days, people often gathered in their homes and apartments to enjoy the opportunity of being introduced to something new in the company of other people. The parties were actually very enjoyable, and we learned to do them. The parties were also rewarding financially as we were able to introduce our products and brand to a group of people. Today, the party or group is more likely to be online whereas geography and time zone difference do not become barriers to participation. We had a lot of fun while we earned "very good money" for the time invested.

VMK was extraordinary, and simply exceptional in her ability to communicate with others, demonstrate products and develop new customers often recruiting them to also become direct sellers with the company that she was involved. As I reflect on VMK, her passion for what she did, and how she accomplished so many goals, ... I remember her always talking about the business that she was building. She was never in it for short-term objectives. Consequently VMK never quit.

When I became an executive at a major direct selling company which I will identify later in this book, I had the pleasure of inviting VMK to look at what we were doing. VMK and her husband took a look, and they became new direct sellers all over again. They joined the company with the same mindset; they would build a business and that is exactly what they did.

Today, VMK remains active with her direct selling business which is now managed more by her children and grandchildren. Her direct selling business is a "business." VMK is considered a very successful direct seller by anyone's standards. She is also considered a legend by anyone who has had the pleasure of knowing her and/or working with her. VMK's direct selling experience exceeds **60 years,** and she remains active with her current company, along with her children and grandchildren. **VMK has been with her current direct selling company for 36 years.**

VMK is an Independent Entrepreneur!

I also had the pleasure of meeting and getting to know LW, a woman who had been an executive assistant (if I remember correctly) in a traditional type of business before she became a direct seller. I had heard a lot about LW before I met her. When we met, I found one of the most authentic, down-to-earth, personable, and fun-loving individuals I had ever met. When I learned more about how she was building her direct selling business, it was obvious that she was very motivated by the idea of "building a business" with an established brand. Most direct sellers work at the endeavor for short term objectives.

LW's mother was viewed as her business partner. The more LW shared her direct selling activities with me, the more impressed I became. Having been successful at direct selling myself, I knew the importance of the personal marketing effort which we often referred to as "sharing." It did not take long for me to realize that LW was a very savvy personal marketer. LW and her mother were doing things I had never thought of doing. LW was so passionate about her company and the brand that she had her car completely wrapped with the brand identity of the company she represented. I know that Joyce and I would never have done that.

LW and her mother were turning their direct selling efforts into a business. They became known for their personalized and creative communications with customers and team members. Those communications touched the lives of many. Today, LW continues to build and manage her direct selling business. She has been with her direct selling company for 39 years. Her success is also legendary. She continues to be an accomplished communicator and has written at least one book, a fictional story that actually represents a lot of her individual experiences.

LW is an independent Entrepreneur!

PERSPECTIVE #2
Successful Direct Sellers Promote the Brand

This perspective is based upon personal experience. Several Direct Selling Companies have become established and well recognized brands that consumers have heard about even when they may not have personally experienced the brand. Most direct selling companies offer brands that consumers may not be aware of however, the common denominator with companies that choose the direct selling channel of distribution is the commitment to quality and price/value.

The direct seller benefits from the company who creates the brand and takes responsibility for the creation of the products/services and the primary marketing effort. The direct seller, the intermediary, is offered the opportunity to represent and promote a brand that has already been created. The direct seller actually enhances the value of the brand when they add a personalized marketing effort based upon personal experience.

Unique brands are continuously created. The internet makes it possible to introduce a brand, in a more personalized manner, without investing the money required when introducing a brand in more traditional retail venues. Direct selling companies invest the expense of brand building essentials into those who represent the brand in a personalized manner. The direct seller no longer purchases inventory to serve customers or marketing materials that are often offered free via the digital platform provided by the direct selling company.

Our first direct selling experience was with a company and brand of which we had never heard. Because we were personally introduced to the company by someone who had personally experienced the brand, we wanted to use the products. After using them ourselves, we too became brand enthusiasts and advocates! We were proud to represent that brand and others felt our authenticity and enthusiasm.

The marketplace now purchases products and services differently. Online/eCommerce is growing at a very robust pace. Globally, eCommerce sales are expected to reach 6 Trillion+ by end of 2025, a growth rate of approximately 8% over prior year. Direct sellers are expected to benefit from these trends as digital platforms become our stores.

Direct Selling Compensation Plans Are Unique

Direct selling companies, generally, offer a unique method of compensation whereas increased performance generally increases the reward. Most direct sellers have short-term objectives. Less than 8% build their direct selling business as a full-time effort. Incremental income is the objective of most direct sellers. The opportunity to share the products and services the direct seller loves that cannot be found through traditional retail outlets makes a direct selling opportunity very unique.

Direct sellers who add a personalized approach to the manner in which they share, represent, and sell the products/services/possibilities they represent, actually create a distinct competitive advantage. We as consumers always appreciate the product or service more when the intermediary adds to the value of the relationship.

From this perspective, it is an oversight to underestimate the opportunity to be rewarded for the continuous purchasing activity of a consumer. All businesses exist and thrive based on the number of customers/clients served. Personally, I am not aware of a business model that succeeds without a growing customer/consumer base. Therefore, direct sellers who promote their brand, who also realize the opportunity to continuously benefit from the relationships they facilitate, appear to be more successful over a longer period of time.

I have been a participant in the direct selling business model, an executive who participated in the growth of specific direct selling business models, author of many articles on various aspects of the direct selling business model, researcher and lifelong student of business models that embrace the involvement of independent contractors. I have designed and participated in the implementation of recognition and rewards programs to support direct sellers who are responsible for new customer acquisition along with the recruitment activities associated with growing the number of distribution points through the attraction of more new direct sellers who duplicate the behaviors described.

The goals of direct sellers are always diverse and very personal. Through all of the experiences that I have mentioned, **I have never found the components of a compensation plan to be more important than the quality and value of the brand or the quality of the relationship the direct seller develops with their customers and other direct sellers.**

The tagline of both books we have authored express the priorities we have found to be most important: **FLEXIBILITY – FREEDOM – REWARDS.** A *NEW ECONOMY* brand provides all three.

PERSPECTIVE #3
Direct Sellers Represent a Significant Segment of Gig Workers and Independent Entrepreneurs

The research conducted by Ultimate Gig Research Project found, contrary to widespread belief that Ride Sharing/Transportation Services/Delivery Services constituted a very significant segment of gig workers, there are other segments that are very strong. Each survey conducted between 2021 – 2023, utilized **Qualtrics Global Online Research Group** for implementation of the surveys. Panels ranged from 1,000 to 2,000 participants representing a solid statistical sample of those participating in the gig economy. Dr. Robert A. Peterson and John T. Fleming led the development of all questions utilized in the surveys conducted.

The Ultimate Gig Project had one primary objective: To better understand the attraction and growth of the gig economy, therefore, we did not offer guidance to Qualtrics as to how panels would be selected. Those who participated in the surveys volunteered as self-declared gig workers. Our methodology in developing the approach to questions and subsets of questions, and our subsequent analysis of survey findings, remains of the more valid and comprehensive studies on the gig economy over the past few years.

At the end of 2024, various estimates related to the size of the gig economy indicated that gig worker participation to be around **70 million**. The **U.S. Direct Selling Association** released in it's **2023 Industry Overview** the following significant statement:

Direct Selling in the United States represents $36.7 billion in retail sales in 2023. In addition there were **37.7 million customers who were served** and **6.1 million direct sellers.** By dividing the $36.7 billion in sales by the 6.1 million direct sellers in 2023, direct sellers averaged $6,016 in retail sales in 2023.

The majority of the direct sellers, 5.6 million, were noted as part-time direct sellers. Gender participation revealed 74% women and 26% men. 15% were in age group 25 -34 and 66% in age groups 25 − 64.

Participation in The Gig Economy by Selected Categories U.G. Survey Results 2023 (A few selected categories)

Type of Gig (Primary Only)	2023 Survey Response (%)
Ridesharing/Transportation	8.2
Delivery Services	13.3*
Child/Elder Care	7.2
Selling Products Services You Make Yourself	12.6
Home Repair/Manual Skills	12.6
Professional Services/Freelancing	11.9
Pet Care/Personal Services	10.1
Selling Products or Services but not direct selling	4.9
Renting Assets	2.2
Selling or representing a direct selling company	2.3**

*Largest single category reported by survey participants.

** Perhaps, direct sellers do not recognize themselves as gig workers?

Note: At the time the U.S. Direct Selling data was released, direct selling models, overall, were in the middle of innovation and renovation, adapting to vast improvements in technology related tools and support, including the emergence of AI. The shift in marketplace/consumer attitudes and behaviors also required attention.

Ultimate Gig Research probed behaviors of the gig worker, their motivations, and their choices of gig work. Simplicity in how work could be done and engaged became obvious to us as a major reason the gig economy had become very appealing to so many. With the support of companies that invested heavily in their technology platforms, often connecting the worker/freelancer with those who need a product or service, the gig economy has grown at consistent and incredible year over year growth rates. These growth rates, previously mentioned, are expected to continue over the next few years as we transition to a *NEW ECONOMY*.

From this perspective, one of the most significant reasons for exploring a direct selling possibility is: There is no need for an independent worker/independent entrepreneur to build a brand. The brand already exists. While this is true in the gig economy, the direct seller engages to leverage their personal assets of love for the product or service to add value to the relationship with both customers and other direct sellers.

The direct selling approach to compensating direct sellers includes continuing rewards for enhancing a relationship with both customers and other direct sellers and maintaining those relationships. Consequently, the direct seller owns (in essence) part of the relationship as long as they are active direct sellers themselves.

The approach to compensation and rewards will differ amongst direct selling companies depending upon products and services provided. Most important is always a program of fair rewards for behaviors which grow the brand, customers, and new points of distribution, for both company and independent direct seller.

Based upon the generally accepted reporting on the size of the Gig Economy and the data released by the U.S. Direct Selling Association for 2023, direct sellers represent a very significant segment of independent workers and independent entrepreneurs (6.1 Million) representing 8.7% of the estimated 70,000 reported gig workers. This statement is provided only as insight.

This perspective summarizes why we encourage exploration of direct selling for both complementary and longer-term income possibilities.

PROSPECTIVE #4
The Future of Direct Selling
Contributed by Deborah Heisz
(Former Direct Selling Executive)

The entrepreneurial dream is alive and well in the United States—but the way people pursue that dream is changing. The new economy has transformed how we think about work, flexibility, and ownership. As a result, anyone considering an entrepreneurial path must look closely at which opportunities truly offer freedom, purpose, and growth. One of the most proven yet misunderstood paths is **direct selling.**

If you've ever wanted to build something of your own, earn extra income on your schedule, or find meaningful work outside of traditional corporate life, direct selling has long provided a low-cost way to do exactly that. For more than a century, direct selling has offered an accessible entry point into entrepreneurship—complete with training, mentorship, and a built-in community of people on the same journey.

But today's world gives you more choices than ever. The spirit of entrepreneurship hasn't changed, but the pathways to it have multiplied. The rise of digital platforms has redefined how people think about freedom, flexibility, and control of their time. Gig-economy possibilities make it easy to earn on demand, however, there is a trade-off. is clear: Easy to engage quick income possibilities, generally, do not offer any form of longer-term ownership. A quick solution is not always a lasting venture.

Online opportunities like Shopify, Etsy, or affiliate marketing can seem appealing too—you can build a store, sell your creations, or share products you love. However, each of these paths comes with its own hurdles: driving traffic, managing shipping, learning algorithms, and staying ahead of constant platform changes. Even with AI tools, standing out in the digital crowd takes time, skill, and capital.

Direct selling, however, has quietly evolved to meet modern entrepreneurs where they are. Long term business building remains a focus and so is the residual income possibility. Direct selling companies also attract and embrace those seeking incremental income and flexible ways to engage. You can start because you love a product, want to share it with friends, or simply need a little extra income—and grow from there at your own pace. Many of the most successful people in direct selling began exactly that way: they didn't set out to build an empire; they just followed their enthusiasm and found a community that supported them.

If you're considering entrepreneurship, look closely at what direct selling offers. Most direct selling companies provide everything you need to operate a business from day one:

- **High-demand products** that people genuinely want to buy.

- **Fair, transparent compensation** that rewards sales of product as much or more than building a team.

- **Immediate, meaningful income** that makes early effort worthwhile.

- **Professional e-commerce systems** that feel as simple and secure as your favorite online stores.

- **Comprehensive training and mentorship** to help you grow your confidence and skills.

In short, direct selling companies remove the hardest parts of starting a business—so you can focus on what matters most: sharing something you believe in.

What makes direct selling especially appealing for modern entrepreneurs is its **flexibility**. You can build your business however it fits into your life. Maybe you'll share your favorite products with friends and family, host small gatherings, or talk about them on social media. Maybe you'll treat it like a part-time passion—or decide to turn it into a full-time career. The beauty of this model is that *you* decide what success looks like.

Direct selling opportunities don't leave you on your own. It's built on **community**—people who want you to succeed. You'll find mentors, training, recognition, and friendship along the way. That sense of belonging is something most side hustles can't offer. In a world where so much work happens behind screens, it's refreshing to be part of something human.

If you're evaluating opportunities, here are a few principles that matter in today's marketplace:

- Choose a company built around products with real consumer demand—not hype.

- Look for a compensation plan that's simple and rewarding from the start.

- Make sure customers (not just sellers) are buying and loving the product.

- Ensure the online shopping experience is easy, safe, and familiar.

- And most importantly, align with a company whose values and community inspire you.

You don't have to choose between flexibility and purpose, or between independence and support. Most direct selling companies deliver all of these attributes in one model—something no app-based gig or influencer platform can truly replicate.

The modern workforce is blending multiple income streams, and direct selling fits perfectly into that reality. Whether you're looking for a meaningful side business or a career with growth potential, you can build at your own pace. The path forward isn't about promises of future payoff; it's about *reward for your effort today*—clear, fair, and worth your time.

Through all the technological changes, one thing hasn't changed: direct selling is, at its heart, a people business. It thrives on human connection, mentorship, collaboration, and celebrating each other's wins. And that is exactly what makes it so relevant in our digital age.

Summary

I've spent years watching the direct selling business model reinvent itself with one constant: the power of ordinary people doing extraordinary things when given a platform and belief in themselves. That's what direct selling has always been about.

When technology, transparency, and authentic connection work together, direct selling becomes the most human form of commerce in a digital world—where entrepreneurship feels personal, purpose-driven, and possible for everyone.

If you're looking for a place to start your entrepreneurial journey, maybe this is it. Because when you combine the freedom to dream with the support to grow, the possibilities are limitless—and the best days of direct selling are still ahead.

CHAPTER 8
THE VOICES—LIVES CHANGED/FUTURES BUILT
Kate Gardner

T his chapter is about the people, in their own words, who are choosing to be in control of their living and working. A *NEW ECONOMY* is emerging where flexibility and freedom become strong attributes. However, there are many who have recognized a desire for more flexibility and freedom in how they live and work who may be considered the original pioneers of the *NEW ECONOMY.*

This chapter unites the voices of people from all walks of life who chose to say "yes" to opportunities and possibilities that were very different from that of a traditional job. Each testimony is a unique reflection of individual dreams, challenges, and triumphs, all with a common thread ... belief in a new possibility and ultimately in themselves. The decision to do something different often marks the

159

moment when ordinary lives take extraordinary turns, whether it's earning a little extra grocery money, building a legacy, or finding the courage to step outside a comfort zone.

What I asked of each storyteller:

1. Why they chose their business

2. What is their degree of satisfaction

Here's my story to set the stage. I followed in the dainty footsteps of Mrs. P.F.E. Albee, the very first Avon Representative, who, in the late 1800's at the age of 50, was "peddling" perfume door-to-door!

> *"In the late 70's my son was barely a toddler. I loved my 'mom mantle' ... however, it did not take long to realize that play time and conversations with my favorite tiny person was simply not enough validation or intellectual stimulation! What I began to look forward to were the bi-weekly visits from my A-Lady ... a lovely, savvy woman who rang my doorbell, carrying a basket filled with the latest in cosmetics and skin care demonstration products!*

> *It was actually my husband who said ... 'you can do that'! So, I did! My 'why' was simple. Yep ... get me out of the house, for starters! AND ... the product aligned with my sense of self. Looking good, feeling pretty was a joyful message to share with so many women in my territory who were also stay-at-home moms! Remember, we're talking the late 70's. Doesn't sound like that many years ago and yet, it was a time when women were home more than working outside the home. The doorbell was almost always answered. I have friends to this day ... and bonus ... so does my son! Those stay-at-home moms had kids just like me! All that ... and an income that met my personal objectives!*

> *Was I satisfied? Totally ... and I continue to be satisfied with that decision to this day. My company's executives recognized this*

successful, basket-toting, doorbell-ringing 'Lady' by bringing her into management! Following some superb graduate school level business and management training, I was assigned to an inner-city market in the heart of Ft. Worth, Texas. Together, with 100's of devoted Independent Reps, we took our district to tops in the nation, Circle of Excellence.

So, almost 50 years later, my first direct selling venture, set my course for a life-long journey in the world of entrepreneurship and business ownership where I continue to thrive and feel relevant to this day!"

It's noteworthy here to share that 'satisfaction' in the business of direct selling rarely stops at income. For many, it's the satisfaction of personal growth, recognition, new friendships, and a renewed sense of purpose.

Each story included in this chapter was gathered with a single intention ... instilling belief in the possibilities represented in this new era of "work" ... a *NEW ECONOMY* in which you can participate and flourish separately or in conjunction with regular work/career.

The stories we've assembled are unique. Many of these stories feature direct sellers across the US and around the world. We chose them because direct selling, perhaps more so than most business models, requires mostly a desire to share with others something embraced that one also loves. My granddaughter included her voice as a reminder that the spirit of entrepreneurship is timeless. Whether 19 or 90, the courage to share your gifts with the world transcends generations. As you read, attempt to identify who my granddaughter might be.

Enjoy these lively testimonials and listen for the passion they have for their products/services; their personal growth in self-confidence and self-reliance, and of course ... the ability to earn an income that meet their needs.

Real Stories/Real People

In my late 20s, I had what many would call 'success' — a steady job, praise for my health focus, and the "look" I thought I was supposed to have. But inside, I kept asking, "Is this it? My weeks felt unfulfilling … 5 AM workouts, long hours spent outside of my calling in the office, meal prep, rinse, and repeat. Weekends were for checking out in unhealthy ways. I wanted more.

Looking back, I can see God's plan was already unfolding. My first job out of college didn't have a strong onboarding system, so I asked to help improve the training, and eventually began training others because people saw that gift in me. Growing up as a dancer made performing and public speaking feel natural, even exciting! Those small moments taught me how to create, lead, and show up without asking permission.

A personalized, DNA-linked health assessment became the fork in the road. It didn't just change my habits; it changed my career. I met strong, committed, faith-filled women - first online and later in person - who modeled a unique way … life-first business, not hustle-first. They believed in me before I believed in myself. Bringing my husband to that first event sealed it! Our founder modeled faith and freedom, and I finally felt called to step into who I was created to be.

Now, my husband and I are growing our family through adoption which is a huge part of our "why." I'm still working on control and perfectionism, but I've found joy in building a business that aligns with my health, my faith, and my family while leading a team across the nation. I'm grateful, still growing, and wholeheartedly convinced, more than ever that freedom + purpose combined with leading others into possibility through my faith - is the point.

—Emily S.

My passion for entrepreneurship started early in life. I grew up with parents who owned a small business, and from them I learned the absolute necessity of putting in the work combined with the value and importance of building relationships. They showed me that success is not simply about selling a product ... it is about creating trust, connection, and community with those whose lives you touch.

Over the years, direct sales has taught me discipline, consistency, and resilience. I live by the motto "you work hard, you play hard," and I was always taught that the worst thing you can do is nothing. Taking action, even imperfect action, is what moves you forward.

There are opportunities at every turn ... what lights you up? What would you be enthusiastic about sharing, promoting, and selling?

I started my direct selling journey with just a sample set plus a little curiosity. Mostly, I wanted a discount on great products. What I found was so much more than amazing skin care, it was confidence, community, and a business I never knew I needed. Four years later, my business has given me lifelong friendships, trips I only dreamed of, and the chance to help others feel their best.

My direct selling company isn't just a business for me — it's a platform for me to empower others, to show that when you pair determination with heart, you can create freedom, fulfillment, a life you love and an income that continues to support my dreams and goals!

—Amy M.

When I found myself in the new role of mother, faced with working full-time and needing to find day care for my son, I recruited myself into direct selling over 22 years ago. That quickly grew to be a welcome addition to our family's bottom line as well as some fantastic travel incentives and an abundance of new friends through my team and wonderful customers.

My direct selling journey began in jewelry and accessories with a company that found it necessary to close its doors. During that time, I had been introduced to another direct selling company's skin care & cosmetics products and had enjoyed many of them for more than a decade. For over 30 years I had struggled with cystic acne and oily, blemished skin. Nothing worked so well at nourishing and treating my skin as their products still do!

In an inspired moment, I reached out to the company asking to speak with the founders or a field development person so I could find out more about their culture and determine if it would be a good fit for us both. What I found after one visit to the home office was all I needed to be "all in" with the authenticity, mission, and future of my new business adventure.

As women we wear many hats . . . wife, mother, daughter, caregiver and so much more. Life can deliver some really challenging ups and downs. This experience with my direct selling company has helped to strengthen my self-care journey combined with informing and encouraging me to help others do the same.

It's been a privilege to grow personally alongside some truly remarkable women. They have put their faith and trust in building a team together with me. And we have a wonderful network of loyal customers all over the country. When thinking back on my years in direct selling, I can't imagine doing anything else with such purpose, passion, and flexibility.

—Jennifer S.

My direct selling adventure has been epic and far more than I could ever imagined. When I first joined my company, it was simply for the product discount on items I loved and they worked! What began as a small step quickly turned into a life-changing journey!

Direct selling gave me the opportunity to build a business on my own terms, fueled by passion, persistence, and community. Over time, my "side gig" quickly grew into a successful business that not only provided financial success, but also incredible personal growth. I always worked hard and smart and I earned many rewards including the use of a company car and a lot of free travel. Most importantly I met many inspiring women and men who became lifelong friends and mentors.

My journey included leadership roles where I had the privilege of coaching and developing leaders across multiple markets. Each milestone—whether personal or professional—has reinforced my belief that the direct selling channel is a very real path to entrepreneurship. It's flexible, boundless, and deeply rewarding - not just in what you achieve, but also in who you become.

Looking back, what started with a love for products became a business that shaped every part of my life. Direct selling enabled me to move from being solely a curious shopper seeking savings into an entrepreneur empowered to help others achieve their desired level of success. This gave me confidence, freedom, adventure, and the joy of seeing others achieve. It proved to me that entrepreneurship transcends boardroom or a big investment - it begins, as it did for me with something as simple as loving a product and sharing it with others. For those who harbor even the smallest spark of ambition, direct selling can be a beacon of opportunity.

—Allison W.

I grew up in a household where goals weren't just talked about — they were pursued with intention and strategy. With a hospital administrator on one side and a financial planner/Dale Carnegie instructor on the other, I learned early on that success wasn't about luck — it was about vision, discipline, and taking action.

One of the most valuable lessons I absorbed was this: high achievers set the goal first — then reverse engineer the strategy to get there. That mindset shaped how I view opportunity, and it's one of the main reasons I chose Direct Sales. This business model rewards initiative, consistency, and a willingness to grow — all qualities my upbringing instilled in me.

What drew me in further was the low-to-no risk of entry. It's one of the few business models where you can build a business without massive overhead, inventory, or complicated startup costs. Even better, you get to choose a company that aligns with your values — from the products and programs to the leadership and culture.

For me, that alignment came naturally in the health and fitness industry, where I found a perfect fit thanks to my ice hockey background and lifelong passion for helping others reach their potential. Direct Sales gave me a way to monetize that passion — to turn what I love into something that impacts lives and generates real income.

With a direct selling opportunity you are rewarded for your authenticity, the relationships you build, and the community you create.

—Mark M.

I was a mom of two little ones, looking for an opportunity that would provide some income, discounts on products I love and use, and some much needed "adult conversation." I had recently quit my job of seven years in finance. I no longer felt appreciated and had to fight to take vacations. Thinking that sales could be the perfect in-between jobs option, I joined my company and committed to attend all offered classes, and training meetings. Oh, my goodness! The recognition, the mega successful direct sellers in the room, their level of joy ... I was instantly blown away! To myself, I said; "If they can do it, I can do it!"

I became totally involved in sales and recruitment and was quickly noticed by my Division Manager who offered me a full-time position. I stepped into management for a few years, loved it, learned a lot, and then guess what I realized? I was right back in where I was originally ... working extreme hours and losing my freedom, flexibility, and family time. I returned to my independent representative status!

I recall friends, colleagues, and family, thinking that I must be crazy to exchange a "secure income" plus a company car, trips, benefits, etc., to be in business for myself. My fondest memories include the recognition my team members have received and the personal recognition that I have received for our performance. My family members are often in attendance - including my daughter, sister, brother-in-law, nieces, and nephew.

I have been very fulfilled with direct sales and all that it has provided for my family and me, not only financially. It has given me an extended family with my teammates and customers. It has been a "business college" that has taught me so much. The number one being BELIEF IN SELF. I believe because of the people who believed in me. It's a business that "Pays Forward."

What I learned and experienced with my direct selling company paved the way for my venture into my other passion. For 20 years, my husband and I have owned and managed a 9-unit historic home that has been an Inn as well as a "home away from home" for traveling professionals worldwide, all while having a successful direct selling business!

I am certain that one can achieve great heights in direct sales and complete satisfaction when the company you select has fantastic, affordable products, a caring and inclusive "culture," incentives, challenging but realistic growth opportunities. It's a win for everyone involved!

—Sandra D.

When I first stepped into direct sales, it wasn't about building a business. Personal health issues had made me more aware of what I was putting on and in my body. As a stay-at-home mom to two-year-old triplets, I was desperate for something to help my skin and to give me back a piece of myself. I loved being a mom, but I had lost the woman I was before. What started as curiosity quickly became something much bigger.

The products are wonderful, but the true gift was the community I found. At a time when my world revolved around toddlers, I felt so isolated. Once I engaged with my direct selling company, I was surrounded by other women who saw me, supported me, and reminded me I wasn't alone. When I walked through two heartbreaking miscarriages, they carried me with love and prayer. These friendships became my safe place and my greatest blessing. I cannot imagine my life without them, and without direct sales I never would have found this kind of connection.

What surprised me most was realizing I could actually be an entrepreneur! I never thought someone like me, home with three little ones, could create consistent income for my family. But my company gave me that chance. I get to call the shots, build my business the way that works for my life, and know that the effort I put in truly matters. I'm my own boss, but I'm never doing it alone. That balance of freedom and support has been life-changing, and it's something I never knew I was capable of until now.

My direct selling experience has been more than the income that I earn. The experience has enhanced my confidence, purpose, and the friendships that have forever changed the course of my life.

—Tricia W.

Authenticity is one of my deepest values, and I worried that if I stepped into sales, I'd have to leave my integrity at the door. The last thing I wanted was to be another "pushy salesperson."

What changed everything was something very personal ... my son's long-term skin sensitivities. When nothing else worked, my mother-in-law gave me a set of products. I tried them reluctantly, but they made a real difference for him. That's when it clicked for me ... if something this effective could help my child, the most authentic choice I could make was to share it with others.

At first, I thought I was just saying yes to helping people with their skin. What surprised me was how much the decision helped me. I found growth I didn't know I needed. I became more confident, resilient, and even began to take better care of myself. Direct selling became more than a part-time business. It became a way of life that let me build connection, creativity, and purpose while still being present with my family.

One of the most powerful parts of the direct selling business model is the acceptance of every type personality. You don't have to fit a mold, you just have to show up as yourself. Not everyone wants the same kind of salesperson, and that's the beauty of it.

Today, I'm more than satisfied. I've built a business that feels aligned with who I am. It is authentic, sustainable, and full of heart. Direct selling has given me the freedom to grow, the platform to encourage others, and the reminder that even in business, integrity and impact can go hand in hand.

—Mandie M.

Throughout my 20 years in Texas, I have been plagued with seasonal allergies. Then in early 2024 a good friend of mine, a nutritionist, introduced me to my nutritional supplements and wellness company.

That's when I learned something simple AND powerful ... sound nutrition in combination with a supplement regimen is integral to healthy living.

At the same time, I began my new supplement regimen, my husband announced he wanted to lose weight. With the help of supplemental nutrition, we both began to experience results.

Our results were visually evident and made for an easily shared conversation with family and friends who also began experiencing the changes they were seeking.

Prior to my direct selling experience, I worked as a banker at one of the largest banks in the world. There I felt like I was only 'trading my time for money,' at the expense of my health, both physical and mental.

The founder of my company is the inspiration behind the scientifically sound products I take and represent. His purpose and commitment inspire my trust and enthusiasm for our products. The education, training and support provided by my company, empowered me to believe in myself and take advantage of the income options available. I have been honored for accomplishments I did not believe possible. It goes beyond just my own health and having a supplemental income.

My journey with my company has only just begun. I have a greater purpose in sharing the vision and products I represent … this is my passion for the rest of my life.

—Jenny C.

Following graduation from college with a bachelor's degree in business, I pursued a career in corporate America, then married and had a son! Like so many working women, I was gutted every time I kissed my son goodbye as I dropped him off at daycare.

Upon becoming a single mother, the hours I carried to meet the demands of my corporate career made it impossible to care for my son. He spent a year living with his dad, which was the worst year of my life.

That year of heart ache was followed by 6 years of stay-at-home-mom joy when I re-married and walked away from my corporate job. Our family grew to 3 children, and we found ourselves in the position of needing extra income. Thus began my search for something I could do to generate income that wouldn't take me away from my children.

Enter direct selling. I got it ... I immediately understood how direct selling provided me the flexibility I required in my family circumstance ... the selling part and income followed.

Direct selling is one of the few income-generating business platforms where you have uncapped earning potential without the requirement of specific education or experience.

You must commit to the work. When you are willing to do that, you can build a life you may have only dreamed of. With direct selling I broke out of a job and started my own business allowing me to set the hours needed to achieve my goals and not miss a moment of my children's lives!

—Christy R.

When I first started with my direct selling company, my "why" was simple. I had quit my teaching job to homeschool my three daughters, and I wanted to save money on products that I already loved. At that time, I never imagined this choice would change so much in my life.

I was shy and scared to reach out to people. I expanded my comfort zone one nervous step at a time, and my confidence grew. I began earning extra income I wasn't expecting, and that helped give my family more opportunities to do fun things together.

My direct selling company experience also helped me find my voice and my confidence. That growth carried into other areas of my life. I started to dream. For years I had thought of fastpacking - think ultralight backpacking but running instead of hiking. I was scared to go solo, but now I had no excuse to put off this dream any longer because I now had the extra income to get the gear I needed. I courageously took my first solo fastpacking trip and fell in love with it and a new passion was born.

I started taking other women under my wing and taught them how to fastpack too. I just launched my own business where I guide women on fastpacking and ultralight backpacking trips. Starting my own business is something I never would have had the courage to pursue if I hadn't first stepped into direct sales. What began with a simple discount for my family has transformed into a journey of growth, confidence, income, adventure, and has put me on a mission of not just helping people with their skin, but to help them grow confident in themselves and encouraging them to pursue their dreams.

—Laura H.

I arrived in the UK from the Philippines in 2000 with one suitcase, £40 in my pocket, and a dream that felt bigger than the city itself. Like many immigrants, I had to start from scratch, but I was determined to build a better life. I studied nursing. Becoming a scrub nurse, anesthetic nurse, then ultimately a Cardiac Surgical Care Practitioner. On the outside, it looked like success ... but the reality was far from easy.

My wife and I worked long hours and extra shifts just to survive. Even with our specialist incomes, we were in debt, often relying on credit cards to get by. We had a full-time nanny looking after our children. One night we realized our eldest son was speaking more Polish than our own language because he spent more time with her than with us! That hit me hard. I suddenly saw the price we were paying for our careers. We were missing the joy of raising our own children.

In 2009, I found my financial services direct selling opportunity. I didn't have much spare time, but I knew I had to try. For five years I built the business part time. Many late nights, sacrifices, and setbacks were part of the journey. Then, one thing changed everything ... leadership. Learning to lead ... not just for myself but for others ... became the key to my growth and success.

On December 26th, 2014, I made what many called a "mad decision". I left the nursing career I had worked so hard to build, to go full time with my direct selling company. It was scary, but looking back, it was the best decision I ever made. Today, as an established direct seller, I control my time, am building a legacy for my family, and we help many others in their efforts to achieve more financial freedom.

—Arvin B.

When I graduated high school in 2017, I had no clear idea of what I wanted to do with my life. I tried college a few times, but nothing seemed to stick, and I floated from one job to another, everything from Pizza Hut to Walmart Corporate e-commerce, searching for something that felt meaningful.

After a cross-country move and some major life changes, I found myself working retail, and it hit me how desperately I needed an education and a new path forward. Going back to school full-time was a turning point for me, but it also meant that I no longer had a conventional job to rely on. That was when I turned to something I had always loved, crafting.

Crochet had always been a creative outlet, but suddenly it became a way to support myself, a way to turn my passion into something that could actually sustain me. What surprised me most was how deeply satisfying it is to see people appreciate the pieces I make and to know they are willing to spend their hard-earned money on something I poured hours of work and care into.

It gives me a sense of accomplishment I had never experienced in my other jobs, where my efforts were often overlooked or credited to someone higher up. This work is different. It is personal. Each piece I create carries a little bit of me in it, and when someone picks it up, smiles, and decides to take it home, it feels like they're saying they see me, not just my product. That connection makes me proud, it motivates me to keep going, and it reminds me that I am building something meaningful for myself and for the people who value my work.

—Tori G.

For more than a decade, I was a loyal consumer of my company's product. My journey began due to a painful struggle with a chronic skin condition. I had tried so many solutions without success. When these products worked for me, it became a lifestyle. Over time, incorporating my wellness routine felt as natural as brushing my teeth.

Over time I became a mother of four and I chose to leave my career and dedicate myself to being a stay-at-home mom. My days were filled with feeding, cooking, cleaning, and putting the kids to bed. It was a beautiful life in many ways, but slowly, I began to realize something ... while I was pouring everything into my children, I was losing myself. My phone was filled with their photos, their milestones, their achievements, but I had none of my own.

Don't get me wrong, I love being a mom with all my heart. But I also knew that my children were watching me closely. And what they saw was a mom who had stopped growing. A mom who didn't take on new challenges. A mom who seemed to have no drive. That realization shook me deeply. I didn't want to raise my children to believe that parenthood meant the end of my personal growth and dreams.

So, I gave myself a challenge ... one year. One year to step out of my comfort zone. One year to give my best effort as an entrepreneur. My logic was simple ... if I fail, at least I'll know I gave it my all. And if I succeed, I'll discover a new version of myself.

I already trusted my company and its products. What I needed was to start believing in myself. And what unfolded in that year was more than I could have imagined. Yes, the income, the travel, the awards, and the recognition were incredibly rewarding. But the greatest reward was my personal growth.

I learned to speak to people with confidence. I learned to face challenges instead of hiding from them. I learned to inspire others who, like me, felt stuck between motherhood and self-growth.

And the best part? My kids saw it all. They now see a mom who is not only loving but also growing, learning, and leading by example. They see a mom who chooses courage. A mom who shows them that life is about constant growth.

And that, to me, is the greatest achievement of all.

—Laura C.

Final Thoughts By Kate

Perhaps as you read, you saw yourself, or maybe you caught a glimpse of who you could become. That's the true power of testimony … it invites us not just to listen, but to imagine!

Did you find yourself leaning into the possibilities of being in business for yourself and not by yourself? We hope that your confidence in yourself has grown as a result of the stories that we have shared. Business opportunities and possibilities are not to be evaluated on traditional logic, stats, or facts alone. This book has presented to you a balance of what is considered most important to your pursuit of your personal goals and objectives.

The stories that we shared included a defining moment when the story teller realized that they too could make something happen in their life that had not been happening prior. The possibilities and opportunities in the *NEW ECONOMY* have never been greater for those who recognize the possibilities.

We hope this chapter may have ignited your defining moment!

CHAPTER 9
ABOUT THE AUTHORS
SUMMARY THOUGHTS/INSIGHTS/OUTLOOK

John T. Fleming
Author
Ultimate Gig, NEW ECONOMY

I have always embraced the belief that being the first to do something different is always a choice. My parents, both educators, encouraged a belief that you accomplish what you think you can. This belief is foundational to everything I have ever accomplished especially my journey from a focus on architecture to direct selling entrepreneur, to corporate executive/officer, publisher, to principal of Ideas & Design Group, LLC, and Project Lead – *Ultimate Gig* Project.

I also recognize the importance of balance in the life/work ... I enjoy work very much so I work a lot at something. Our research on the phenomenal growth of the gig economy simply strengthened my long-held position on the value of personal growth and development, and empowering others through our personal performance behaviors. Below is a personal belief:

> *"Flexibility and freedom in how work can be accomplished is our new reality for all segments in society. Companies that support strong principles, values, ethics, and the personal development and success of their workers – employee or independent contractor, in managing work/ life, will also experience increases in productivity, worker satisfaction and growth which will be win-win."*

Author's Personal Background/Perspectives

My life and work have always been about the journey--not any particular destination. As I conceived the ideas surrounding this book, I wanted to share some of my personal thoughts and make them available to others. I was not interested in attempting to inspire or motivate, only present insights and perspectives. I never looked for the instant fix to any challenge, nor was I ever impressed with what someone else had accomplished even though some of the accomplishments were impressive. I never wanted to be like someone else, only to be the best that I could be—myself. I always found enthusiasm in learning and doing.

I have learned that it is hard to self-evaluate but easy to lose the desired feeling of satisfaction and self-confidence, making it harder to deal with fear of the unknown or the challenge of change. I have learned to embrace the opportunity to learn and am committed to being a student forever. I look forward to the possibilities. By focusing on possibilities it becomes harder to remain satisfied for too long because we quickly realize that "better" is always a possibility.

Seven distinct phases characterize my life and work. I would like to share why I think this personal reflection and perspective may add value to what you, the reader, might gain from the sharing of my thoughts.

Learning The Importance Of Relevance

1. **Growing Up.** Life is so very exciting when we are growing up because we are a shared responsibility between parents, family, guardians, or a community. My biggest challenges were to have fun, keep my room clean, study, get good grades, grow up, seek post-secondary education, get an excellent job, find a partner, start a family and be a productive citizen in the community. I always wanted to be an architect and my definition and understanding of an architect was that of understanding that an architect designs buildings...very cool buildings, and I wanted to be someone who designed buildings. I wanted to be relevant.

2. **Architectural School.** Because I had done well with the early childhood challenges and followed the basic rules, I attracted the attention of others who wanted to see me become as relevant as I could. An excellent high school counselor coached me and mentored me. I was accepted into one of the best engineering schools in the country. **We learned quickly in architectural school that all designs don't get built, and those that are built are built to last.**

   I thrived on the concepts taught in architectural school along with learning the integral importance of engineering to good architectural design. A building is built upon solid concepts, principles, and even laws of physics and structure. This has been true, actually for a few thousand years and, consequently, some of the great structures designed and built a few thousand years ago still stand to some degree. I learned such structures were not built on ideas and emotion alone, they were built using principles and engineering concepts.

   Looking back, it's amazing how architectural school taught me so much about living and working in general. As architecture students, we never considered design and building from the point of view that we might create something irrelevant. The young men and women who could not grasp this basic thought simply were not around at the beginning of the sophomore year.

With the passage of time, buildings do become irrelevant and when they become irrelevant, we tear them down and build new ones, or we renovate. It's a very simple philosophy that we learn and accept. No one seems to want a house without plumbing anymore. We all expect indoor plumbing, modern conveniences, a building that is efficient in design and the manner in which it serves our needs. We seek relevance and do not approve of irrelevance....at least when it comes to structures designed and built to serve us.

3. **Working in the office of Mies Van der Rohe.** Ludwig Mies van der Rohe - world-renowned architect, founded the School of Architecture at Illinois Institute of Technology (IIT). As a student at IIT, I continued to attract the interest of others. It was not my grades alone. Performance, I now realized, was also very important. As a student, I was invited to work full-time in the Office of Mies van der Rohe during my first summer break and part-time during the school semesters. I got paid; I was not simply an intern in the office of one of the world's most renowned architects. When Swiss author Werner Blazer was approved and authorized by Mies to author the last book to be written about him in his lifetime, I was selected to do the illustrations for the book. This responsibility included recreating a few drawings that Mies had originally drawn himself. I will never forget the opportunity to interact directly with Mies. Even though the personal time was very limited, it only took a few minutes for him to explain the purpose and reasoning for the drawings he wanted to replicate in the book. Mies Van der Rohe is typically recognized as one the three masters of contemporary architecture. The other two are Le Corbusier and Frank Lloyd Wright.

On occasion, Mies would invite the office team to his home for pizza and beverages on Friday evening. The informal conversations often went into the morning hours. We would sit on the floor most of the time and listen to Mies talk for hours…. He shared his purpose, his philosophies, and he never wavered from his beliefs in "Less is More," "Form follows Function," and "God is in the details." Mies always intended to be one of the most relevant architects ever, and that is exactly what he became.

4. **Engagement of a direct selling opportunity changed my life and my focus on the type of work that I enjoyed.** When I first made the decision to embrace a direct selling opportunity very seriously, the questions were many and they often sounded like this: **You are doing what????** My sponsor in direct sales, Mr. Willie Larkin is actually the person who changed my outlook on how I might serve others in a very different manner… how Joyce and I might build a business, one step at a time, without disruption to our core careers. It worked.

   Even though I was now becoming a believer and advocate of the direct selling model, my foundational commitments to always being relevant were simply transferred. The principles that I had learned relating to the design and construction of buildings remained integral to my core philosophical beliefs.

5. **Avon Products, Inc.** changed my life again. Having met Rick Goings, now CEO Emeritus, Tupperware Brands, who was president of Avon North America at that time and becoming friends with Rick through **Direct Selling Association** meetings, ended up being more valuable than I could ever have imagined. I remember the call I received from Rick inviting me to visit him in New York City at Avon Headquarters. He explained an Avon project designed to "contemporize" Avon and prepare the brand for its next 100 years. I was not that familiar with the word "contemporize" at that time. Today, I would simply use the word transformation. The project was more than

exciting. I made a few more trips to New York to meet other members of the Avon Executive Team. As I developed a clear idea of what might be possible, I knew that I had been a good student of direct selling and understood the principles and values which Avon always kept at the forefront. I also knew that Joyce and I had learned how to build a solid direct selling business, and we had become very successful at doing it by our own standards. I do not remember the exact moment the offer came from Avon to join the executive team, but I do remember acknowledging that I would respond quickly. My biggest question was whether Joyce was willing to move to New York City, and the answer was "no." Fortunately, Avon never made the move an issue and I joined the Super Bowl winning team of what was, at that time, the largest direct selling brand in the world.

I quickly became Vice President of Sales Contemporization at Avon with the responsibility of leading the Transformation Team. I worked with all of the key executives, which was a most exhilarating and meaningful era in my growth – personally and professionally. Avon was, at that time, recognizing and rewarding Avon Representatives via a single level approach to compensation supported by excellent recognition for performance. Avon Representatives represented women from all walks of life. The focus of our project was to enhance the way Avon Representatives were recognized and rewarded while maintaining a focus on simplicity vs complexity. We introduced new concepts quickly, deliberately, and methodically. Our strategic planning was solid to allow the new Contemporized Avon to thrive without disrupting the "grand ol' lady" – the Avon company already in existence. When we rolled out the new plans, throughout the United States, we quickly gained "buy-in" because we had thought it through and developed real examples along the way. My leadership was focused on performance, not theory; therefore, I personally engaged in attracting excellent direct selling examples to the updated version of Avon. We made it clear to those within Avon that our transformation effort was designed to support the next 100 years. We attracted those from within the company and a few from outside the company who were intrigued by what was happening at Avon.

I learned great lessons about the importance of relevance. Avon had always been inclusive of men in the executive ranks but being relevant for me also meant, most importantly, being perceived as relevant by Avon Representatives - the ladies who carried the Avon torch. I had planned to be at Avon for two or three years. I was there for 15 years. I remained for as long as I did because I was perceived to be relevant, and I perceived our company to be a relevant force of good for women throughout the world. Those were amazing times at Avon ... I learned a lot about the importance of relevancy.

Direct Selling News. Things changed at Avon, and I chose an early retirement opportunity. Many have asked me why I left, and my response is quite simple; it was time for me to do more of what I wanted to do.... to become even more relevant. My reasons for leaving Avon are a bit more than I am willing to express here, perhaps another story at another time.

Stuart Johnson, founder of Video Plus, SUCCESS Partners and Direct Selling News offered me an opportunity, ... one that kept me growing and provided me an opportunity to increase my relevance. I had no desire to work for another company or for someone else and Stuart made something very special possible. Stuart had launched *Direct Selling News*, a monthly publication for direct selling executives. The publication was focused on serving executives, not the direct sellers who actually sold products. While most industries had invested in such a publication, there was no monthly trade association publication serving direct selling executives. Stuart wanted to build such a publication. Stuart invited me to join in his efforts to build the *Direct Selling News* brand.

I accepted Stuart's offer and challenge to take over the leadership of the effort to build a trade publication focused on serving direct selling executives. I over promised that I thought that we could become profitable very quickly. I knew nothing about journalism; however, Stuart already had a talented team in place and that was all we needed. Deborah Heisz was the first publisher of *Direct Selling News*. I knew that we could build upon what had been started. Our initial focus on positive journalism supportive of clarifying and defining the direct selling business model worked well.

I also knew was that it was all about "team" and staying focused on what matters most—what is most relevant to the audience. Stuart allowed us to stay focused on relevance, not profits, by paying the bills. We attracted advertisers and some remain with *Direct Selling News* today. Nacy Laichas was the first editor at *Direct Selling News*. I took the title (self-anointed) Publisher, Editor-in-Chief. However, it was Nancy who knew how to get a publication done, and she did so month after month, and we grew. We focused on being relevant.

Jerry Reagan led the quest for advertisers. Jerry was an aspiring pastor, who did not want a job. He really wanted to serve a congregation. Jerry only wanted to help people, and he was the perfect person to be in charge of advertising at *Direct Selling News* because he caught the vision and only wanted to tell the story in a personal manner. Jerry knew that we needed revenue, but his approach was to sell the vision, the purpose of what we were attempting to do in building a relevant publication to serve direct selling executives was what made him so successful. This was the relevant approach to seeking advertisers.

Erica Jennings was the first graphic artist. She helped us to immediately transform the image of the publication, and we became more relevant quickly. Rebecca Larson wrote many of the first articles establishing the importance of substance in the article vs allowing companies to self-promote when we selected them for inclusion in the publication. The strategy worked.

Eventually, we started to break even, but more importantly we built a relevant brand. When Stuart paid the bills that we could not bear solely ourselves, I always knew that Stuart was investing in relevance. Based upon that foundational focus, we transformed the 8-page, two color, newsletter into a sustainable and growing brand which today is the premier publication and media platform serving direct selling executives.

When I took the challenge Stuart offered, I had planned to stay two to three years, but I remained Publisher/Editor in Chief for nine years. I loved what we were doing. Stuart started something of immense importance, and I was delighted to be a part of something that was relevant!

Ideas and Design Group, LLC (IDG) & Black Educational Events, LLC (BEE). When I left Avon, I knew that I would do some consulting/advising. I also knew that I wanted to experiment with doing something entrepreneurial with my son. We experimented with a few things, the most memorable of which are the experiences gained from forming Black Educational Events, LLC, producing an extensive Resource Guide on Historically Black Colleges and Universities (HBCUs), and producing what became one of the Top 5 HBCU College Football Classics in the nation - *The Angel City Classic*. We produced the classic for 3 years; the final year being broadcast live on Fox Sports West. The Angel City Classic was held in the Los Angeles Coliseum. The attendance hit 55,000 in our last year of production. Each year, we made it possible for the entire football team, coaches, key faculty, cheerleaders, entire band, and dance teams, to bring their talents to Los Angeles California to showcase them in an area, where the public knew very little about the Historically Black College/University experience.

My son and I, with no experience in producing events, attracted and built a team that produced excellent marketing, public relations, sponsorship acquisition, contract negotiation with major venues including airlines, and services of all types. The events were focused on educating a portion of Los Angeles via showcasing students in the form of a football game along with a team of cheerleaders and dancers, and the talents of the band. The common denominator – all of the students were pursuing post-secondary education at a

Historically Black College/University. We were not into producing a football game. We were simply displaying talented students through a football game and ancillary events, which were wrapped into a full day of activities. The attendees and the City of Los Angeles consistently referred to the Angel City Classic as an experience much greater than a game. We had produced a successful event, a relevant event, but not a successful project financially. There were external circumstances that we could not control in 2008, the last event we produced. I now view the experience as being a paradoxical experience. We were relevant but not successful.

Even though I founded Ideas & Design Group, LLC (IDG) immediately after I left Avon, I was never really interested in being a consultant. I have been choosing who I work with. I have always thought of IDG as more of a "think tank" provoking thought— strategic thoughts and ideas relative to the concepts of simplicity vs complexity, as well as how "less can be more." The experiences gained at Avon - leading, and collaborating with a transformative team, and achieving incredible success at that time, was proof of concept as to how transformation and change can be approached, embraced, and executed. Consequently, the relationships I've built have given me a unique window into strategic thinking at its finest.

One project born of relationship building is The *Ultimate Gig* Project. Approximately 7 years ago, I recognized a changing trend relative to how we work. Work flexibility was becoming increasingly appealing and out of nowhere the gig economy seemed to emerge in popularity, attracting all segments of the population to flexible work opportunities. I was both fascinated and amazed. How and why did part-time work opportunities become so popular? The emergence of the pandemic further changed societal expectations of what work looks like. Technology provided us with greater ability to do more with less. New visionaries and analytical thinkers created new opportunities within the gig economy, whereas under-utilized personal assets in the form of physical assets, knowledge, experience, skills, passion, and purpose could be leveraged to build an income stream through various new types of opportunities.

We learned from our research studies between 2020 and 2025, all led by Dr. Robert A. Peterson, University of Texas, Austin: Direct selling, as a channel of distribution, should be explored. The gig economy continues to attract those seeking opportunities and possibilities to enhance income or work differently. Various business models are in a moment much like the moments faced or not faced by Kroger, the A&P Grocery Chain of stores, Kodak, Block Buster, J.C. Penny, Sears Roebuck, and many others. Jim Collins interviews with Kroger CEO's most responsible for their transformation and success decades ago shows that these executives felt they had done nothing particularly special. They had studied the data and applied strategic thinking to create new plans for the future. Kroger Grocery Stores continue to thrive today.

Personal Recognition. Recognition is the result of performance or contribution. Recognition in a sports activity also recognizes the success of a team. I categorize all recognition that I have ever received to be an honor received on behalf of the many people that I have attempted to serve and sometimes inspire to be high performers in what I describe as a high-performance culture. This applies to every job (there were only a few), and every project that I have ever been engaged in. The recognition received includes:

> **Avon West Tiffany Crystal Eagle Sculpture** (18-1/2" high, gold claws on the eagle with inscription – *"He taught is how to soar"*). Avon West was the #1. Performing business unit for six consecutive years in a row in Avon North America.

> Direct Selling Education Foundation **Circle of Honor**

> Direct Selling Association **Hall of Fame**

> Direct Selling News **Lifetime Achiever**

> Direct Selling News **Legends Recognition**

Perhaps, the awards and recognition received indicates that there are others who desired to recognize my relevance. If so, it makes me happy. My intention, through all of my work has always been focused on the effort, the performance, and the contributions that I could make to serve others.

I hope that my sharing may stimulate your sharing with others your greatness in whatever form that may be. It is indeed a beautiful world, and the opportunities and possibilities have never been greater however challenging they may appear to be at times. Our work and projects will continue to support efforts related to conveying the value of individual entrepreneurship.

Last Words/Personal Thoughts

From my experience, what is most important is the impact that we as individuals have on others, beyond what we achieve or how we are perceived. Our growth, sustained relevance, and sustained winning is most important to us personally and to those who live and work alongside us because everything we do or don't do ripples to impact the larger whole. That said, the summary or outcome of this chapter is really up to you. You will summarize your personal thoughts. This means that it is very important to step outside the "sand box" you may be in and become a student; read, study, develop questions, pursue your view of the future and how you will participate. Challenging ourselves to be better, to grow and thrive, and to win at whatever it is that we have chosen to do appears to be essential to avoiding any symptoms of irrelevance… at least that is my perspective.

Outlook

My optimism always trumps concern or skepticism. Opportunities to transform and change should never be taken for granted or taken lightly. Winners not only survive; they thrive, regardless of the difficulty or the challenge. Challenges and difficulties seem to have minimal impact on those determined to win. The winners in the *NEW ECONOMY* will be those from all walks of life who do their personal research, study, and bring forth the best of personal decisions as to what matters most … personally.

In *NEW ECONOMY* we have presented an optimistic view. Our economy is definitely more inclusive, and workers have much more of an opportunity to own a portion of the work if not the entirety of the work. The *NEW ECONOMY* emerges in the midst of what many may describe as challenging times. The *NEW ECONOMY* will be more about the number of opportunities and possibilities!

Robert A. Peterson

D r. Robert A. Peterson is the John T. Stuart III Centennial Chair in Business (Emeritus) at The University of Texas at Austin. His professional career spans more than half a century. In addition to his role as a marketing professor, Dr. Peterson served as a department chairman, an associate dean, the director of both an institute and a research center, and 10 years as associate vice president at The University of Texas. He has published more than 200 peer-reviewed articles and books; his marketing strategy textbook is currently in its 13th edition and has been adopted globally. His award-winning research encompasses studies focusing on topics in consumer behavior as well as business, including surveys of the gig economy. Among his many academic awards and recognitions is one that stands out: there is a supercomputer in Portugal named in his honor ("Bob").

Dr. Peterson is also an erstwhile entrepreneur, having co-founded four companies and been involved in several startups. In addition, he has served on the boards and executive committees of several corporations and nonprofit associations and institutions as well as advisory committees to the State of Texas and the United States Bureau of the Census. He has consulted with hundreds of companies and governments worldwide and testified as an expert witness in scores of litigation matters involving intellectual property and unfair competition.

Bob and his wife of 60 years Diane have three children and two grandchildren. Among their accomplishments are having played golf in 30 countries and too many states to mention.

Kate Gardner

For almost five decades, Katharine Gardner, Kate to her friends and colleagues, has been a driving force in the direct selling industry - an advisor, leader, and connector whose career is woven into the very fabric of the channel. Today, through Gardner Co LLC dba C3 Executive Search, Kate focuses her energy on resourcing top talent for direct selling companies while continuing to guide colleagues through consulting and peer-learning initiatives.

Kate's story began with a basket of Avon products and a neighborhood route. Those door-to-door days sparked her passion for entrepreneurship and people development, leading her into direct sales management. From there, Kate's career leapt into leadership - most notably as President/COO of Multiples USA, where she pioneered omni-channel strategies long before the term was coined. Live Home Shopping Network appearances, outlet store rollouts, and groundbreaking collaborations showcased her ability to innovate and deliver "never been done before" business expansion solutions.

Her influence has extended well beyond company walls. Kate served multiple terms on the Boards of the Direct Selling Association (DSA) and the Direct Selling Education Foundation (DSEF), chaired the DSA's Member Services Committee, and participated in early efforts to define digital marketing in the industry. She also spearheaded philanthropic initiatives, from Multiples USA's Susan G. Komen Race for the Cure sponsorships to leading the SUCCESS Foundation's global "SUCCESS for Teens" program.

Kate's collaborative spirit continues through ventures like **theJuice**, a peer-learning community for direct selling executives. She also partners with direct selling icon John T. Fleming and Brett Duncan, co-founder of the Juice, to advance thought leadership on the Gig Economy and executive development.

Beyond the boardroom, Kate's heart is with family. She proudly raised her granddaughter Victoria, now studying Environmental Science, and delights in her son Ryan's growing family.

Nestled near Charlottesville, VA, Kate blends her love for business leadership, people, and community with a contagious energy that continues to inspire.

CHAPTER 10
BONUS CHAPTER
STRATEGIC SIMPLICITY FOR INDIVIDUAL ENTREPRENEURS

A Synopsis of Original Work—
Contributed by Tony Jeary

*"You can and should be strategic about everything that matters.
Enjoy More, Impact More, Become More."*

RESULTS Faster! Publishing Info@TonyJeary.com 817.430.9422

Manufactured by MiniBük®, a registered trademark of MiniBük, LLC

ONLY A SELECT FEW...
Tony personally selects only a handful of clients to enter into a "Collaborative Relationship" with, where he and his team pour their energy into Super-Charging their RESULTS!

TONY JEARY
THE RESULTS GUY™
COACH TO THE WORLD'S
TOP COMPANIES, CEOs
AND HIGH ACHIEVERS

A Personal Message From Tony

Often people build too much complexity into their lives, and complexity can pull from their joy and happiness. It can drain the strength that enables them to be their best and impact others.

Living simply brings a balance to our lives. It's more than just a trend called minimalism that might carry its torch for a while and then fade away, as most trends do. I believe we can all benefit from bringing more simplicity to our lives for the long haul.

I read somewhere that living simply creates space to live our truth. I like that. It becomes a matter of capacity. How full is your cup (your space)? When we fill up our calendars, our minds, our cabinets, our closets, and even our down time to the point of overflow, we don't have the space to live out the things that are most important. We become defined by what we do and what we have instead of who we are. Simplicity does create space—space I call "margin time"—for things like serving others, reading, spending time with our families.

So how full is your cup? If it's overflowing, this chapter is for you. You may be stuck in that mode simply because you lack awareness or you have a fuzzy vision, or because of poor decisions you've made. My tagline is **"Change your thinking, change your results."** I believe you can make your life richer and fuller by strategically bringing simplicity to your awareness and taking actions to make it a reality.

On a personal note, with every book I write, I do my best to think through whether I'm personally living out what I'm writing.

Ninety-nine percent of the time I can answer with a resounding yes! Occasionally, though, I ask myself if I can make an impact on my own life by doing more of whatever I'm writing about. Throughout all of my books and teachings, you'll find that I have put in place many processes to simplify my life; however, there's always room for improvement, and **Strategic Simplicity** has become more and more important to me in recent years. As I write this, I can think of several areas in which further simplification would enable me to do more of the things that are important to me. Every reader needs to have that same kind of reflection.

We've divided this work into three sections, and I believe you can be strategic about all three:

•   Defining Simplicity (the What)

•   The Benefits of a Simple Life (the Why)

•   Strategic Actions for Achieving Simplicity (the How)

My life's mission is zeroed in on encouraging people, coaching them to think, and helping them get more of the right RESULTS (the results they want) even faster! My hope is that this bonus chapter, a synopsis of the original mini book will do exactly that for you.

Serving the best, Tony

Let me start by providing you with a few examples from my personal life:

I've made a strategic decision to own only one car. That simplifies my life because I have no car payments. My car is an older model (with low mileage), and yet it looks and runs like it's brand new. I replace my personal vehicle on an average of every six or seven years, compared to most of my peers who do so much more often. Think about the complexities involved with buying a new car:

Among other things, you have to sell or trade in the old car; you have to transfer the insurance from the old car to the new; and you have to change the tags. All of that translates into complexity.

My business vehicle is what we call The RESULTS1 Van. It's a special Mercedes Sprinter van that I had built custom so my drivers could transport our clients when they come in to spend time with me and my team at our RESULTS Studio. I wanted it to provide the "wow factor" for our clients—and it does. And yet I also employed Strategic Simplicity for certain features. Bill Connelly, my best friend for over thirty-five years, has owned a number of larger vehicles for many years, including a Peter Frampton tour bus. When I was having my van built, I went to him for advice. I told him I expected to utilize the vehicle for at least ten years, and he said, "Then build it accordingly." So I did; I built it without electric seats, with hardwood floors instead of carpet, and with minimum electronics and lighting. Then I bought a 100,000-mile warranty and put it into service for our agency. It's simple, yet elegant enough to give our clients a pampered and impressive ride.

I have a very clean, thin, and simple closet, because I constantly give away clothes that I no longer wear and I dress "simply" every day, or most days.

In the late nineties, I had a large, complex business, with offices all over the world. I decided I wanted to strategically invest more time with my kids as they were growing up, so I simplified my life and business by building a private studio on my estate, just a few yards away from my back door. So for the past twenty years, more often than not, my clients have come to me rather than my going to them. (Of course, for this to happen, my agency has needed to provide second-to-none value—real wins my clients could get nowhere else—and we have continued to do that consistently over the years.) I have handpicked a few excellent people to be on my full-time team, and I contract out to another set of highly qualified, handpicked people to ensure we get things done fast for our clients, who love speed. I've done this intentionally while still creating an above-average income and net worth, and the benefits of my simpler life have been too many to count. (In order to keep my life simple, though, I still have to be smart every day about saying no, reducing clutter and obligations, and aligning with my values.) Perhaps you, too, could simplify your life drastically by intentionally and strategically trimming down your obligations, your operation, and your "stuff."

Years ago I learned that it is better to buy quality, not quantity— that it was best to have fewer things that were of superior quality than to have a lot of things that were of second-rate quality. Even though I'm not sure I've lived that out as well as I could have in the past, I focus on that filter now more than ever because I can see real value in simplifying my life with that tenet. In short, Strategic Simplicity comes in many shapes and sizes. It's just a matter of finding the best fit for you and your family.

The Benefits of a Simple Life (the Why)

You may want to employ Strategic Simplicity as a reaction to negative things in your life like materialism, constant consumption, exhaustion from having to manage or even think about so many things, or the realization that you don't own your life. (I call that living on a hamster wheel. Is that where you live? If so, you're in big company; millions of people live there!)

Or you can strategically choose simple living for a variety of other personal reasons. You may make the choice for spiritual reasons, or you may want to improve your health by having less stress. Perhaps you want to do as I did many years ago, increase your quality time with your family and really pour into your kids intentionally. (I think that's a big one

for most people. I know it is for me. As I write this, I've set a new goal to spend more time with my mom. It's not that I can't; it's just a matter of how complicated I make my life.) Maybe you long for a more reasonable work/ life balance, or it may be that your personal taste tends to lean more toward simplicity and frugality. Personally, all those reasons have wins.

I mentioned margin time earlier. I first heard that term years ago from a client in Canada. When she mentioned it to me, it had an enormous impact. Margin time is something we all want more of—to be able to put a vacation, a fun activity with our kids, or just time to sit and think or read or pray on our calendar and then be able to do it. Or we may want more time to take care of our health. Many of the clients we work with want to see their children more, or they want to travel more, and yet they can't because their lives are too complex. There are many wins from the margin time that can come with Strategic Simplicity.

More Benefits of Strategic Simplicity

Consider these three additional benefits of a simpler life:

Healthier Life—Simple living can benefit physical and mental health on many levels. According to the CDC, more people die today from largely preventable diseases, such as high blood pressure and diabetes, than from infectious diseases. The simple lifestyle can incorporate eating fresh, unprocessed, more natural foods that help people stay healthier longer. Living a simpler life also helps lower stress, which naturally decreases blood pressure, and reduces risk of disease, migraines, and colds.

Time for Fun and Laughter—Cutting back the stress in our lives gives more time to relax and have fun. At the end of life what do you want to remember—the long hours working or the fun times with family and friends? Living simply allows for more balance in life, which makes it easier to maintain the lifestyle we desire and acquire more good memories.

Less Clutter, More Organized—Living simply declutters a daily schedule and materialistic lifestyle. Simplifying gives us the ability to eliminate stuff such as activities, chores, responsibilities, and clutter around the house. It gives us room to breathe and relax without feeling over- whelmed and pressured from the noise of life.

I'm so blessed to be able to love what I do every day— impact peoples' lives. If working is a pleasure for you like it is for me, we certainly don't want to ignore that. (If your work can be your hobby, then you truly have a vocation versus a job or even a career.) We do, however, encourage you to think, audit, and consider ways you can simplify your work life, whether that involves some of the things we've mentioned or other things you can do to reduce stress and create more margin time.

One thing I teach is that we all have 168 hours a week, and when you take out 56 for sleeping and 12 for maintenance, which leaves 100 hours to be split between professional and personal activities. Most people would normally split those 100 hours 50/50; however, in your quest for Strategic Simplicity, you can change that ratio to anything your situation allows—maybe 40/60 (40 professional and 60 personal) or even 30/70 or less if that's what simplicity means to you. Or maybe you can even overlap the two areas if your professional activities are more like a personal hobby for you. (For example, I'd rather write a book, give a speech, or coach a high achiever than play golf—and I have truly enjoyed playing golf since I was nine.)

Invisible Benefits of Living Simply

In addition to the visible benefits of Strategic Simplicity (less clutter, less furniture, less "stuff"), we've mentioned a few "invisible" benefits as well, like a healthier life, more time for fun and laughter, a more dedicated spiritual walk, and more margin time. Actually, the invisible benefits are perhaps the most valuable of all. Here are a few more:

- **Giving** – When we simplify our lives, it takes less to make us happy; and when we have margin time to think about the things that really matter, we become more loving, caring, and giving.

- **More Thoughtful Reactions** – A simpler life allows for time to consider a better response when things go wrong. When things are too hectic and complicated, we are more reactionary, say things we don't mean, and blow things out of proportion.

- **Self-Care** – When we reduce commitments, obligations, and as many stressors as possible, there is more time to relax, think, pray, be creative, and be grateful. Some diseases can be caused by stress and exhaustion. Many people tend to abuse themselves with overextension of demanding work in order to succeed. They have a habit of sacrificing not only their physical and emotional health, but other areas of their lives as well, such as family and friends.

- **More Engaged Relationships** – It's often hard to connect with those we love as much as we would like, because we over-complicate our lives. (This is one area I have to constantly work on.) Think about it. Spending more time with those you love can be a pretty powerful benefit.

- **More Capacity** – When we aren't tied to stuff, engaged in drama, or overreacting, we have massive freedom. We make better decisions and are better able to live the lives we truly want. We can be freer to be exactly who we are.

- **Peace, Love, Happiness, and Health** – Without simplicity in our lives, our entire being will be compromised. When we live a hectic lifestyle, we are in a constant battle of striving and never arriving. When we simplify our lives, we live with that inner feeling of peace and contentment with what we have; we have more room for loving others; we have time to reflect on the satisfaction of simple human needs; and we can focus on our mental, spiritual, and physical health.

The invisible benefits of Strategic Simplicity are a giant win.

Strategic Actions for Achieving Simplicity (the How)

Awareness

You must think before you do. All actions—and hence all results—follow thinking. Take the time to reflect and give strong thought to your life and the life you want to live. Is it too complex? Too simple? Chances are, when you answer the previous two questions, your awareness will skyrocket.

After a flood in our home, my wife decided not to replace some things and to simplify others. I have to say, it's very refreshing walking through our home now—I've noticed there are fewer things to get dirty, fewer things to fall, and fewer things to keep up with. That's been an inspiration as we've thought and talked about what we want for the condominium when we move; we're now considering buying nicer things rather than more things. That event really increased our awareness about Strategic Simplicity.

Clarity

After reading this book and gaining more awareness, it's now time to get clearer on what kind of life you want to

live—simple or complex. One fantastic way to do that is to use my concept of MOLO to audit your life.

MOLO

MOLO is a very powerful—and yet very simple—activity that can literally change your life. It's basically eliminating activities you shouldn't be doing. First, you want to determine what you want more of and what you want less of, and then you need to determine what you need to do more of and what you need to do less of in order to get there.

The goal of this tool I invented several years ago is to help you create a better allocation of your time, effort, and resources so you can get greater returns and greater results. (It's about simplicity.) That's what a MOLO audit can do. It can show you where you're wasting your efforts, often in small ways, and complicating your life. And it also can help you get clearer on where you should be investing your time to get more "bang for your buck," so to speak, so you can significantly move the results needle and simplify your life.

(Note: Do a search for "Tony Jeary on MOLO" and watch the short video.)

Conclusion: Simplify Your Life!

You probably know that carrying around extra weight can have negative effects on your health and happiness. Have you ever wondered how all the other "extras" in your life might be affecting you? I hope I've convinced you, as you've read this bonus chapter, that Strategic Simplicity is a real win.

Let me leave you with a story that you may fully relate to, or you may see at least see some similarities to your life.

A successful businessperson had a family with two young children, good health, and all the comforts he wanted a lovely home, new cars every few years, and plenty of discretionary income. One day he looked extremely unhappy, and a friend asked him what was going on. He said he had just seen a family portrait that his eight- year-old daughter had drawn in school. The family was seated around the table eating dinner—and he wasn't in the picture. When he asked his daughter why, she said, "Daddy, you're never home at dinner time. You don't get home until bedtime."

He was devastated. He suddenly felt that everything he had worked so hard to achieve was meaningless—that he had failed his family. Over the next few months, he was able to develop a more balanced perspective and recognize that some things needed to change. His work took way too much of his time and energy, and the material benefits his work provided were turning out to be no substitute for the other things his family needed from him—and no substitute for what he needed from them, either.

The unfortunate thing is that the first part of that story is played out all over the world every day. The fortunate thing is that this man was wise enough to see the truth of what his complex lifestyle was costing him and his family. If you see yourself in this story, I hope you can see that, as well. There are costs and benefits related to everything we do—including everything we agree to do. We must have strategic clarity about what we want, we must be strategic about our focus, and we must execute on what really matters to have our best life.

Remember...

Defining Simplicity (the What)

- Simple living can encompass a number of strategic, voluntary practices that will simplify your lifestyle. It can mean:

- Saying no more often

- Being happy with less—less obligations, less clutter, less everything

- Being more flexible

- Reducing your possessions

- Increasing your self-sufficiency

- Being more satisfied with what you have rather than what you want

- Living simply doesn't mean living in poverty; it's a voluntary lifestyle—choosing to have less, need less, and still live a rich life because of all the benefits it brings.

- Strategic Simplicity comes in many shapes and sizes. It's just a matter of finding the best fit for you and your family.

- The Benefits of a Simpler Life (the Why)

- Margin time. There are many wins from the margin time that can come with Strategic Simplicity. A healthier life. Simple living can benefit physical and mental health on many levels.

- Time for fun and laughter. Cutting back the stress in our lives gives us more time to relax and have fun.

- Less clutter, more organized. Living simply declutters a daily schedule and materialistic lifestyle.

- Giving. When we simplify our lives, it takes less to make us happy; and when we have margin time to think about the things that really matter, we become more loving, caring, and giving.

- More thoughtful reactions. A simpler life allows time to consider a better response when things go wrong.

- Self-care. When we reduce commitments, obligations, and as many stressors as possible, there is more time to relax, think, pray, be creative, and be grateful.

- More engaged relationships. It's often hard to connect with those we love as much as we would like, because we over-complicate our lives.

- More capacity. When we aren't tied to stuff, engaged in drama, or overreacting, we have massive freedom. We make better decisions and are better able to live the lives we truly want.

- Strategic Actions for Achieving Simplicity (the How)

- Awareness. All actions—and hence all results— follow thinking. Take the time to reflect and give strong thought to your life and the life you want to live. Is it too complex? Too simple? Chances are, when you answer those two questions, your awareness will skyrocket.

- Clarity. After reading this book and gaining more awareness, it's now time to get really clear on what kind of life you want to live—simple or complex. One terrific way to do that is to MOLO your life.

- MOLO (More Of Less Of). This powerful activity can show you where you're wasting your efforts, often in small ways, and complicating your life. It can also help you get clearer on where you should be investing your time to significantly move the results needle and simplify your life.

- Focus. Focus will help you identify and concentrate on what matters the most for the success of your vision for a simpler lifestyle, and it will help you filter out distractions that hinder its progress.

- Elimination. Making to-do lists and a list of your goals will simplify your life in a huge way. And taking things off your lists if they no longer matter is crucial.

CHAPTER 11
RECOMMENDED ACTIONS

SUPPORT FOR INDIVIDUAL ENTREPRENEURS

This closing chapter highlights a few services that we recommend based upon personal experience. As technology has evolved to having such a positive impact on every aspect of living and working, Independent Entrepreneurs are encouraged to explore the suggestions carefully.

1. The New Public Library Is The Internet.

With any of the popular search engines, you can search for what you would like to know more about with a few clicks. I am always amazed at how easy it is to search any topic and how quickly I receive the information.

Unlike the public library of past years, we no longer have to go to a physical building and sit for many hours reviewing many books focused on our topic of interest. Most libraries that were housed in a physical building were never full of people yet all of the books that we wanted to review were available "free."

The internet is so much better! We can access information related to just about anything that we can think of at any time, and we can be on a smartphone, tablet, or computer, anywhere. When questions arise in your own thinking, it is suggested that you keep a special set of notes, perhaps noted "Personal Research/Reading." The list includes everything that you thought of that you need to seek more information. This is similar to visiting the library. The difference: you are now able to bring the library to you, on your time, through the internet. You can do your research at the time most convenient to you. This simple activity, equivalent to visiting the library may be one of the most important investments of your own time. I remember distinctly sharing with both of our children, when we dropped them off for their first semester at college: " make the library one of your most favorite places." This was a constant reminder to them of the importance of seeking information and of course, ... study.

2. Video Conferencing Is Essential

In a world being redefined at speeds never experienced, video conferencing eliminates the time zone and geographical barriers typically associated with the type of work that we can engage. A video conference tool enables the Individual entrepreneur the opportunity to engage the customer or client without the need to be physically be present. Video conference tools also support the personal marketing and selling effort.

We recommend that you explore Meetn:
www.meetn.com/safetynetspecial

Here's Why? For entrepreneurs, the world changed the moment "let's hop on a meeting" became as natural as "let's grab coffee." What was once a clunky backup plan when you couldn't meet in person has become the primary tool for all types of businesses, especially the *NEW ECONOMY* Independent Entrepreneur. Online meetings have completely rewritten the playbook for how businesses scale and compete.

Think about it - in the past, flying across the country to attend a meeting or spending hours commuting to a meeting was just part of the business grind. Now, a founder can pitch an investor in the morning, sync with their development team in Bengaluru (Bangalore) at night and still have time for dinner with their family. For the individual entrepreneur, the ability to build relationships regardless of geographical or time zone constraints is the new possibility. Virtual meeting enables the smallest business type, the ability to compete with giants (more established companies).

This speed advantage is important. Startups are naturally accelerationist; always moving, always iterating. Virtual platforms like Meetn, Zoom, Google Meet, Web X, or Teams amplify that by providing virtual meeting tools which connect people very effectively. Web meetings and online workspaces make teams more responsive. No more waiting around for a follow-up meeting in two weeks – individuals and groups can brainstorm, test, and act in real time.

Online meetings also change the way teams are structured by leveling the playing field. On a screen, everyone gets the same size box. This shift supports the flat organizational structures startups thrive on, where knowledge and skills matter more than titles. Smart leaders use this to their advantage, designing virtual meetings to draw out voices that might hesitate to participate in person.

Of course, it's not all upside. Poorly run virtual meetings can hurt productivity if there's no follow-up or clarity afterward. For entrepreneurs, the lesson is clear: online meetings are powerful, but they need structure: agendas, takeaways, and sometimes, the occasional face-to-face moment to recharge the human connection. The next wave of platform innovation addresses these challenges with specialization. Tools like Meetn are built not just to connect people, but to drive outcomes - helping close sales, expand networks, and onboard new hires.

What does this mean for you and your business? For us, it means that a scrappy startup with a webcam and a big idea can go toe-to-toe with industry giants. Online meetings didn't just make communication easier – they have leveled the playing field and sped up the game. The virtual room is no longer merely a tool for business - it *is* business.

Contributed By:

Alan Alpert Founder Smart Office Solutions
Michelle Flick, President Meetn

3. **Bookkeeping Is Essential**

Over many years of personal experience as a Direct Seller and Individual Entrepreneur, I have observed others who did not keep track of income vs expenses. Therefore, tax time always activated stress and frustration vs the opportunity to measure the true effectiveness of the work-related endeavor. Independent Workers are in business for themselves and are entitled to deductions that can be easily overlooked without utilization of a simple and easy to manage book keeping system. **This type of tool should not be overlooked.** Good book keeping ensures compliance with all applicable laws and rules when used consistently and appropriately. There are several systems designed to support individual business owners that are easy to manage. Most will allow you to link directly to bank accounts and credit cards.

We recommend that you explore systems like Wave.

4. Marketing and Campaign Management Is Essential

Many years ago, I adopted the following business building philosophy. When you have something of value to offer others and a commitment to share authentically what you have to offer, you enhance your chances of success by reaching out to others consistently. My strategy, when building a direct selling business, was to simply talk personally to a minimum of 3 people per day, 5 days per week. That strategy worked very well. Fast forward to today. Think about the tools that you now have available to promote what you have to offer. Creating your own campaigns is easy when using tools that help you create and format messages.

We recommend that you explore Trinity & Ignite: www.trinitysoftware.com

5. **Associations and Subscriptions**

Success in any endeavor is generally fueled by association and the community of other like-minded individuals whom we can benefit. The following resources are recommended:

Safety Net Resources—One Time Subscription Fee—$24.95

Safety Net Resources is a digital platform focused on providing simplicity vs complexity when seeking relevant content that supports the mindset of the Individual Entrepreneur. Created by **Ideas & Design Group (IDG)**, a few recommendations are made in four categories of content:

Education—Guidance—Tools—Library

Under each category, selected content and recommendations simplify the process of learning and thinking by identifying "what matters most" in support of the Individual Entrepreneur.

Safety Resources is the exclusive source of *NEW ECONOMY* book in digital format. All subscribers receive a free download of the book which is available in print format via Amazon.

Subscribers can also expect, once a quarter, a free download of a unique article and newsletter created/sourced by the Safety Net Resources team.

We recommend that you explore Safety Net Resources: www.safetynetresource.info

The Association For Entrepreneurship
Membership is $4.99 Per Month

The **Association For Entrepreneurship (AFE)** is focused on supporting the needs of entrepreneurs of all types, especially the new Independent Entrepreneur. The monthly membership fee is less than the cost of a good burger or cup of coffee each month.

Membership includes access to basic health related services. Access to outstanding Insurance Products and Financial Services (A-Tier Carriers), are provided at group rates. Members explore what they need when they need to with the assistance of a licensed professional. Access to these types of products has always been a barrier or obstacle to those seeking to explore Individual Entrepreneurship when they decide to make their gig or small business their full-time career.

We recommend that you explore the Association For Entrepreneurship: www.theultimateresource.info

6. **Health Sharing vs Health Insurance**

Simple, Transparent, Affordable Healthcare

You're building your business, maybe leading a team, and making things happen on a daily basis—healthcare should support you, not create added stress or financial strain.

Impact Health Sharing is a non-insurance, community-focused alternative, built differently on purpose to give health-conscious entrepreneurs, individuals, and families a smarter, more affordable way to manage healthcare.

Why Entrepreneurs Choose Impact:

- **Savings:** Members typically save up to 50% per month on average.

- **Transparent, Family-Friendly Costs:** Clear guidelines, no hidden fees, and for families, one annual responsibility amount per household instead of per person.

- **Rewarded for Living Well:** Earn rewards every month for gym memberships, supplements, acupuncture, and more—helping reduce your annual household amount.

- **Freedom of Choice:** Keep the doctors and providers you trust—no network restrictions and no utilization reviews.

- **Instant Extra Perks & More Savings** (Included): Complimentary 24/7 telehealth, annual wellness visit, prescription, dental and vision savings and more—starting day one, at no additional cost.

- **Secure, Tech-Enabled Platform:** Easily manage your membership and healthcare in one place, while sharing in the community's eligible medical needs are executed securely, seamlessly, and transparently through our online platform.

How It Works:

1. **Get Your Free Quote:** See your personalized pricing in seconds, commitment-free.

2. **Review the Guidelines:** Learn how sharing works and see if it fits your needs.

3. **Enroll:** Start saving while enjoying flexible, comprehensive healthcare supported by a community of people helping people. Enrollment is open year-round. Take charge of your healthcare and related expenses —choose a smarter, affordable, non-profit alternative that puts people first, the way healthcare should be.

We recommend that you explore Health Sharing.

Visit www1.impacthealthsharing.com/neweconomy to get your free, no-commitment quote and to discover if Impact is a fit for you.

"This book has been focused on the growing audience of Independent Entrepreneurs in all formats. We hope that you have benefited from the content of this book.

The focus for this book looked closely at the Situation Analysis in the United States, however, the information, thoughts and perspectives shared, appear to be applicable to mature economies throughout the world.

The future of work defines the future of the world."

—John Fleming

www.ingramcontent.com/pod-product-compliance
Lightning Source LLC
Chambersburg PA
CBHW021759190326
41518CB00007B/376